P9-DIW-346

This book belongs to
CHELSEA CONSTANT

Leading Beyond the Walls

Developing Congregations
with a Heart
for the Unchurched

Adam Hamilton

Foreword by Lyle E. Schaller

Abingdon Press
Nashville

LEADING BEYOND THE WALLS
DEVELOPING CONGREGATIONS WITH A HEART FOR THE
UNCHURCHED

Copyright © 2002 by Abingdon Press

All rights reserved.
No part of this work may be reproduced or transmitted in any form or
by any means, electronic or mechanical, including photocopying and
recording, or by any information storage or retrieval system, except as
may be expressly permitted by the 1976 Copyright Act or in writing from
the publisher. Requests for permission should be addressed to Abingdon
Press, 201 Eighth Avenue South, P.O. Box 801, Nashville, TN 37202-0801.

This book is printed on acid-free paper.

ISBN 0-687-06415-5

Cataloging-in-Publication Data is available from the Library of Congress.

Scripture quotations, unless otherwise indicated, are from the *New Revised Standard Version of the Bible,* copyright © 1989, by the Division of
Christian Education of the National Council of the Churches of Christ
in the United States of America. Used by permission. All rights reserved.

Scripture quotations noted KJV are from the King James Version of
the Bible.

Scripture quotations marked (NIV) are taken from the HOLY BIBLE,
NEW INTERNATIONAL VERSION®. NIV®. Copyright © 1973, 1978,
1984 by International Bible Society. Used by permission of Zondervan
Publishing House. All right reserved.

02 03 04 05 06 07 08 09 10 11— 10 9 8 7 6 5 4 3 2 1

MANUFACTURED IN THE UNITED STATES OF AMERICA

To my wife and partner in ministry, LaVon, and our daughters Danielle and Rebecca, without whom this book could never have been written

And to Phil Hollis, Gary Patterson, and Bob Robertson, three pastors who changed my life

Contents

Foreword

Most of us who grew into adulthood before 1965 were taught that life consists of making either-or choices. The world offers you two choices: take it or leave it. The high school graduate could enter the labor force or enroll in an institution of higher education. You could choose between keeping your old car or trading it in for a new one. When you retired, you could continue to enjoy the summers up North or move to the Sun Belt. A wife could choose between motherhood or a full-time career in the labor force. The new American economy offers millions of people the both-and option.

Adam Hamilton has written the best book I have ever read on how to be an effective parish pastor. Why is it so good? Because it describes how to be a pastor in the twenty-first century, not in the 1950s or 1980s! It is organized around a both-and approach to what traditionally have been identified as either-or questions.

Why do three-quarters of all American Protestant congregations—and 81 percent of all United Methodist churches— report an average worship attendance of fewer than 150, while fewer than 2 percent of these congregations average eight hundred or more at weekly worship?

A standard explanation is small churches prefer a pastor who excels as a loving shepherd, and a worship attendance of 150 is the maximum-size flock for that pastoral role. At the other end of the size spectrum, the very large churches affirm the need for a pastor who fills the role of a visionary leader. That either-or distinction is offered to explain the recent increase in the number of small congregations in American Protestantism, and the doubling during the 1990s in the number of congregations averaging a thousand or more at worship. By their choice in ministerial leadership roles congregations make an either-or decision about their future. This either-or explanation can be supported by the decrease in several denominational families in the number of congregations averaging between one hundred and eighteen hundred at worship.

In a chapter that is worth far more than the cover price of this book, Hamilton explains that in the new ecclesiastical economy this is a both-and issue. A pastor can serve as both a loving shepherd and also fill the role of the visionary leader.

In the old ecclesiastical economy the pastor was assumed to be a "learned person." The combination of a college degree and a seminary education was expected to produce that learned person. Adam Hamilton models the point that the effective pastors of the twenty-first century are lifelong and self-motivated learners.

This book is filled with lessons for ministers who want to be effective parish pastors in the twenty-first century. For example, should a church have a low threshold or a high threshold for those seeking to become members? Hamilton describes this as another both-and issue.

One of the most important lessons is that the old American ecclesiastical culture divided the world between tasks or functions and relationships. "He's a great preacher, but he can't relate to people on a one-to-one basis." "My secretary is great on the telephone, but she can't type an error-free letter."

Hamilton repeatedly describes that it is not only possible to excel in both relationships and functions, but that excellence in tasks also is reinforced by a high level of competence in relationships. Pastors who have served as loving shepherds of small congregations and now are called to be senior ministers of multiple-staff churches often describe the difficulty they have in delegating responsibilities to others. That reflects the old either-or view of the choice between doing or delegating. In his gentle and gracious style, Hamilton redefines the issue from *doing* to making sure it *gets done*.

While at times this founding pastor of one of today's megachurches displays an excessive degree of modesty, the story of The United Methodist Church of the Resurrection affirms three lessons that many denominational leaders prefer to ignore. One lesson is that it is much easier to create and implement a vision of ministry for a new era in a new mission than it is to do that in a tradition-driven congregation that has been in existence for several decades.

A second and less visible lesson is based on the fact that the number of adult believers who are unchurched exceeds the number of nonbelievers in most communities. One of the most effective strategies for reaching those neglected believers is to listen carefully to their stories. Too much of the academic preparation for the parish ministry is organized around communication by reading and talking, rather than by listening. The grading system in schools tends to reward talkers rather than listeners. A central theme in this book is the value of active listening.

A third lesson that Hamilton models reflects a basic guiding generalization: the larger the size of the congregation, the more influential is the role of the senior minister.

Finally, while others often view these as divisive issues, the story of The Church of the Resurrection also includes the importance of an obsession with excellence, the value of creative marketing strategies, the emergence of a culture organized around memorable and meaningful personal experiences, the shift from teaching to learning, and the freedom to raise the old ceilings that formerly limited expectations.

LYLE E. SCHALLER

Preface

This book was written out of a deep longing to see churches, especially mainline churches—which have struggled during the last third of the twentieth century—become vital, alive, and dynamic forces in service to Christ. While the principles and methodologies outlined in this book will work in almost any church setting from Pentecostal to Roman Catholic, my experience in ministry has been within one of the historic mainline churches in America. The last half of the twentieth century saw the fall of mainline churches and the rise of charismatic, nondenominational, and fundamentalist churches. I am persuaded that the first half of the twenty-first century could see the reemergence of the mainline churches.

My experience as senior pastor at The United Methodist Church of the Resurrection is that twenty-first-century people are hungry for a way of doing Christianity that mainline churches have to offer. At Church of the Resurrection, our emphasis on both tradition and relevance; our emphasis on both the experiential as well as the cognitive dimensions of Christian faith; our willingness to deal with the ambiguities and challenges of faith while holding fast to the truth of the gospel; our appreciation for the role of women in the church; and our dual proclamation of both the evangelical and social gospel are the very things twenty-first-century people are longing for.

The ideas presented in this book are not hypothetical. They are based upon the actual experience of ten years of ministry in which a United Methodist church saw unprecedented growth, from four people to over eight thousand children, youth, and adult members. I have often felt as though I were witnessing a contemporary reliving of the Acts of the Apostles. My hope is that this book has captured in a helpful way some of the key elements that have led to this growth.

I want to express my deepest appreciation to my wife, LaVon, and our children, Danielle and Rebecca, who have played a greater role than even they understand in the development of The Church of the Resurrection. My best ideas were either shaped by them or improved by them. They have been my strength, my inspiration, and my joy. LaVon has been my partner, companion, confidante, and friend. She is the most remarkable woman I have ever known.

Words cannot express how grateful I am for the staff, leaders, and laity of The United Methodist Church of the Resurrection. The staff are, I believe, the most incredible team of people to serve any church anywhere. Among this exceptional gathering of people is my executive assistant, Sue Thompson, who has been an invaluable part of my ministry. Few great churches are built without great administrative assistants to the senior pastor and Church of the Resurrection is no exception.

In addition to a wonderful staff, we are gifted at the church with incredible lay leadership. These leaders are deeply committed to Christ and to the mission of the church. Many of them devote fifteen to twenty hours a week to the church, without compensation while working full-time jobs. They are among the brightest, most creative, energetic and gifted people I have ever met. I am so proud of our laypeople at The Church of the Resurrection. They have shaped my life in so many ways, and I thank God every day for the privilege of serving as their pastor.

Finally, I want to express my deepest thanks to Robert Ratcliff, my editor with Abingdon Press, for his encouragement, insight, and support, and to Rene Leath for her outstanding proofreading and editorial work.

May this book be a source of encouragement, ideas, and inspiration as you, the reader, seek to lead your church.

Introduction

For the last thirty-five years mainline churches have experienced a precipitous decline in membership and worship attendance. Many had forecast the death of America's mainline. But as we enter the twenty-first century there are signs, not of death, but of renewal in these churches—as though God's mission for them was not yet complete. Across the country there are United Methodist, Presbyterian, Disciples of Christ, Lutheran, Episcopalian, and other congregations associated with the historic mainline Protestant movement that are seeing tremendous growth in every way—many outpacing their more conservative counterparts in reaching their communities.

Yet while the signs of renewal offer hope, for the vast majority of churches in these denominations the future is still hanging in the balance. Many pastors and laypeople alike want to see their congregations grow. But despite their efforts, results seem elusive. In many cases it is difficult to lead congregations to make the necessary changes that could foster growth. In other cases leaders are uncertain what steps to take. Often what is needed is not a new program, but a renewed vision, and a new way of thinking about and "doing" church.

I believe this book can help those pastors and church leaders who have a desire to see their churches become vital, healthy, and alive. I write not as a theorist, but as one who has actually pastored a mainline church that has experienced incredible growth. In this book I have attempted to outline both the principles and concrete ideas and strategies that have played a role in the growth of The United Methodist Church of the Resurrection—a congregation that began with four people in the summer of 1990 and which, by the end of 2000 had a membership of over 6,000 adults and 2,000 children and an average worship attendance between 5,000 and 6,000 per weekend.

Many will note that starting a new church in a suburban setting is far different from, and many would say easier than, transforming an existing congregation that is experiencing decline. They note that it is easier to "give birth than to raise the dead." But over the last ten years I have had the opportunity to observe many established churches that were once in decline and now are experiencing renewal and growth. Study these churches carefully and you will find many of the same concepts, strategies, and principles outlined in this book. I have shared the ideas in this book in seminars across the country and have been excited to see the results of churches applying them. Again and again I have heard back from pastors and church leaders in small, medium, and large churches who have told me that the strategies and concepts offered on these pages have worked in their churches, often producing dramatic results.

> **While the signs of renewal offer hope, for the vast majority of churches the future is still hanging in the balance.**

My prayer for this book is that it will offer you, the reader, encouragement, insight, and concrete strategies for leading your congregation outside the walls of your church. The foundation for doing this is cultivating in your church a heart for the unchurched.

ONE

A Biblical Model for Leadership: The Shepherd

The purpose of this book is to encourage effective leadership in the local church, which in turn will develop dynamic congregations. The pastor plays a critical role in the leadership and success of the church, so I will begin by focusing on the heart and mission of the pastor. At the same time I will propose that the calling of pastor goes far beyond one single individual in the church and is, in fact, a calling that belongs to all church leaders, lay and clergy.

I'll begin with a simple question: What is a "pastor"? We know what an auto mechanic is. We understand what a dentist does. But what is a pastor? Interestingly enough the word only appears once in the entire Bible, in Ephesians 4:11 where we read of the five (or four, if pastor and teacher are synonymous terms as some suggest) leadership offices of the early church: "It was [God] who gave some to be apostles, some to be prophets, some to be evangelists, and some to be pastors and teachers" (NIV). While the office is assumed throughout the New Testament, it is nowhere else specifically mentioned by name in the Bible.

The etymology of the word, however, would suggest that the idea behind it runs throughout the Scriptures. The word comes from the Latin, from which our word *pasture* also comes. It meant "to feed" and was usually applied to one who took care of animals, particularly sheep. And thus its connection to the word *shepherd*, a word that appears frequently throughout the Bible.

In the Old Testament we learn that God is a shepherd to Israel—tending the Israelite people, providing for them, guiding them, protecting them. But in addition to God's role as the chief shepherd, God appoints and calls certain people to act as shepherds of God's sheep. The concept of leadership was synonymous with shepherding the people of Israel. In Numbers

27:17 we find Joshua being called a "shepherd" as he became Moses' successor. During the period of the judges God considered the tribal leaders shepherds. Later, David himself was called to "shepherd" Israel.

Clearly, shepherd-leaders are important in accomplishing God's purposes in the world, not only in ancient Israel, but to the present day. God can work in amazing ways, but often God's mighty acts are accomplished through leaders, who are willing to act as God's shepherds.

Through the prophets Jeremiah and Ezekiel, however, God condemned the "shepherds of Israel" who failed to care for God's people. Ezekiel 34 demonstrates what God expected of the shepherds by reading what they failed to do:

> Thus says the Lord GOD: Ah, you shepherds of Israel who have been feeding yourselves! Should not shepherds feed the sheep? You eat the fat, you clothe yourselves with the wool, you slaughter the fatlings; but you do not *feed the sheep. You have not strengthened the weak, you have not healed the sick, you have not bound up the injured, you have not brought back the strayed, you have not sought the lost,* but with force and harshness you have ruled them. So they were scattered, because there was no shepherd. (34:2-5, emphasis added)

These shepherds were both the rulers of Israel, and priests and prophets. They had all missed the mark. Later God promises that, "I will place over them one shepherd, my servant David, and he will tend them; he will tend them and be their shepherd" (34:23 NIV). The Gospel writers clearly portray Jesus as fulfilling this prophetic expectation.

Pastors, staff members, and church leaders are among today's shepherds in the church. We are all called to follow in the footsteps of Jesus, the chief shepherd, who demonstrates to us what shepherding is meant to look like.

Both the heart of Jesus and his ministry are summarized for us in Matthew 9:35-38:

> Then Jesus *went* about all the cities and villages, *teaching* in their synagogues, and *proclaiming* the good news of the kingdom, and *curing* every disease and every sickness. When he *saw* the crowds, he had *compassion* for them, because they were

harassed and helpless, like sheep without a shepherd. Then he said to his disciples, "The harvest is plentiful, but the laborers are few; therefore ask the Lord of the harvest to send out laborers into his harvest." (emphasis added)

Notice what this passage teaches us about Jesus' ministry: First, he went where the people were and did not wait for them to come to him. Just as he approached Zacchaeus in the sycamore tree, or ate in the homes of "sinners," Jesus did not wait for people to come to him. He took the initiative to go to those who were lost. Shepherds go to where the sheep are.

This is a key role of the church leader. We are to develop relationships with sheep, both those in our flock and those who are lost. We are to go to where they live, where they work, where they are. This includes the obvious pastoral calls to the hospitals, visitation in our members' homes when there is a death or a trauma, and follow-up with the unchurched who visit our churches. But it goes beyond this. Church leaders and pastors are to go into the community, getting to know and building relationships with unchurched people and caring for those who are hurting. For some this may mean joining a civic group, or volunteering in the schools, or serving on a board or agency that is not related to the church. For some it will be volunteering in inner-city ministries or working in the prisons. One pastor I know became the captain of the local volunteer fire department. This resulted in ministry opportunities with lost persons that few pastors could even imagine.

> **Church leaders and pastors are to go into the community, getting to know and building relationships with unchurched people and caring for those who are hurting.**

Notice in our passage from Matthew 9 that Jesus' ministry involved teaching, preaching, and healing. As we know from reading the Gospels Jesus taught and preached by using stories that nominally religious people would understand. He preached "good news," words of encouragement and hope for people who were oppressed. And he healed broken people, those who were physically, emotionally, and spiritually wounded. Church leaders and pastors are to be about these same ministries today.

Verse 36 is profound in that it notes two characteristics of Jesus' ministry. First, Jesus *saw* the crowds. He looked at these people and didn't see them simply as masses, or as irritants, but saw them as human beings, as the very reason for his ministry. I have heard pastors say, only half-jokingly, "I would love being a pastor were it not for having to work with people!" I understand the humor and have felt this way myself at times. But Jesus, despite being constantly surrounded by people who each wanted a small piece of him, still looked at these masses and saw them as individual people who were loved by God. The second thing I love about this verse is it reveals the heart of Jesus, for when he saw the people, he had *compassion* for them, for they were like "sheep without a shepherd."

We frequently have people attend our church who do things that are troubling. Some are rude to our staff. I have received several reports of persons offering certain inappropriate hand gestures as they fight for parking spaces on Sunday morning. Some let their children cry in worship. One Sunday we found a vial of cocaine that had fallen to the floor in one of our rooms. Don't misunderstand, most people don't act this way at our church, but each one who does is a visible reminder that the church is reaching lost people, for lost people act lost! Their lives have not been transformed by Christ yet. But when you demonstrate compassion and care for these sheep, loving them and gently offering them Christ, amazing things can happen. This is the role of biblical shepherds, both pastors and church leaders.

In Luke 15:4-7 Jesus leads us even farther down this path when he tells the parable of the lost sheep. Notice the heart and the actions of the shepherd:

> "Which one of you, having a hundred sheep and losing one
> of them, does not leave the ninety-nine in the wilderness and
> go after the one that is lost until he finds it? When he has found
> it, he lays it on his shoulders and rejoices. And when he comes
> home, he calls together his friends and neighbors, saying to

them, 'Rejoice with me, for I have found my sheep that was lost.' Just so, I tell you, there will be more joy in heaven over one sinner who repents than over ninety-nine righteous persons who need no repentance."

The shepherd rejoices at finding the lost sheep! And when he comes home he calls together all of his friends to celebrate! Imagine the church where all of the members celebrate every time another lost sheep comes back to the fold! That is exactly what Jesus tells us is the case in heaven. Once more we discover that shepherds who follow in the footsteps of Jesus are those who have a heart for lost sheep. I've mentioned this already in the passage from Ezekiel, but it runs throughout the ministry of Jesus. As I will note elsewhere in this book, Jesus was quite clear about his ministry when he said in Luke 19:10 (a passage every church leader should have committed to memory), "The Son of Man came to seek out and to save the lost."

In John 10 Jesus offers the wonderful discourse in which he tells us he is the "good shepherd." His words paint a picture for us of the difference between a hired hand and a true shepherd,

> "I am the good shepherd. The good shepherd lays down his life for the sheep. The hired hand, who is not the shepherd and does not own the sheep, sees the wolf coming and leaves the sheep and runs away—and the wolf snatches them and scatters them. The hired hand runs away because a hired hand does not care for the sheep. I am the good shepherd. I know my own and my own know me, just as the Father knows me and I know the Father. And I lay down my life for the sheep." (vv. 11-15)

At times pastors and church leaders can see themselves as "hired hands" but the true shepherds look at the sheep from God's perspective—we love them, feel responsible for them, seek to protect them, and we will sometimes make significant sacrifices for them. In fact, it is often our acts of sacrificial love on their behalf that inspire the sheep to follow our leadership.

Among the last of the Gospel passages, we read of Peter's reinstatement following Christ's resurrection in John 21. Here Jesus asks Peter three times, "Do you love me?" When Peter responds in the affirmative, Jesus gives him his commission: "If you love me then <u>feed my lambs</u>; <u>tend my sheep</u>; <u>feed my lambs</u>" (see vv. 15-17). This passage clearly links our love for Christ to our work as shepherds. Our work in caring for and feeding the sheep is an expression of our love for Christ; our work is an act of worship.

The shepherding role of the church is not simply relegated to the senior pastor, but is shared by all leaders of the church. Senior pastors play a critical role, and this book is written in part for them. But every leader in the church should be seeking to shepherd the flock. Paul the apostle captures this in his final words to the leaders of the church at Ephesus in Acts 20:28. Here Paul addresses the "overseers" or "elders." These titles were used to describe all of the leaders of this church, not simply the pastor, if indeed they had just one pastor. Note what Paul says to these leaders in Acts 20:28, "Keep watch over yourselves and over all the flock, of which the Holy Spirit has made you overseers, *to shepherd* the church of God that he obtained with the blood of his own Son" (emphasis added).

> **Jesus was quite clear about his ministry when he said, "The Son of Man came to seek out and to save the lost."**

Our role, then, as church leaders, is to shepherd God's flock as we seek, in the words of Ezekiel, to "<u>feed the sheep</u>, <u>strengthen the weak, heal the sick, bind up the injured, bring back the strayed</u>, and seek the lost."

The remainder of this book will seek to offer insights, ideas, and strategies for how you as shepherds can effectively discharge these responsibilities, and in the process, develop local congregations that are alive, dynamic, and able to transform your community and world for Christ.

TWO

Three Questions You Must Answer

In 1990 I was sent as a mission pastor to start a new congregation in the south part of the Kansas City metropolitan area. I remember spending the summer before we launched Church of the Resurrection wrestling with three questions:

1. Why do people need Christ?
2. Why do people need the church?
3. Why do they need *this particular* church?

Without an answer a church will flounder. Without deep conviction about the responses to these questions, a pastor will never lead a congregation to change the world. But when a pastor, a church leader, or a congregation is clear about the answers, and able to inspire others about the answers to these questions, the power of the church begins to be unleashed.

I'd like to take a few moments to consider the answers to these three questions.

Why Do People Need Christ?

Why do people need Christ? This question strikes at the very heart of the Christian faith. Your picture of who Jesus is will determine in large part how you answer this question. The New Testament offers us a multitude of portraits of Jesus that together help us understand his identity. He is the Son of God, the promised Messiah, the Good Shepherd, and the Savior who lays down his life for the sins of the world. He is the Resurrected Lord, demonstrating his power over sin and death. He rules and reigns in the hearts of his followers and in God's kingdom eternal. He is the "image of the invisible God," and the Word made flesh. He is the way, the truth, and the life. And these are just a handful of the biblical pictures of the identity of Jesus.

Though you may clearly articulate a biblical Christology, you still cannot answer this question until you consider the human condition. This question is first a question about human need and the human condition. Why do we need what Jesus offers? To answer this question one could spend a lifetime studying sociology and cultural anthropology. Or you can read the newspaper, watch the news, get to know people, and understand yourself. Here's a bit of what you may discover:

The deepest problems facing our society are, at core, spiritual problems. We read of teenagers killing one another and know that a society that produces an increasing number of these kids is in trouble. What is wrong with us and how might Christ be a part of God's solution? We live in a world consumed with possessions; people often go to any lengths to "gain the whole world." How does faith in Christ help people not to lose their souls in such a world? A young gay college student is beaten to death by his fellow students. An epidemic of compulsive gambling follows the wave of new riverboats in town. Racism divides a city. What is the answer? Is it more legislation, tougher laws, more police, or lawyers or judges? Perhaps, but the real solution must address the condition of the human heart; it must break hearts of stone, transform hate into love, and offer healing and deliverance to those who are slaves to ideas, or their upbringing, or their addictions.

> **Jesus Christ is the solution to the deepest longings of the human heart. He is the answer to the most serious problems that plague our society.**

Now, here's the conviction that I came to be seized by: Jesus Christ is the solution to the deepest longings of the human heart. He is the answer to the most serious problems that plague our society. When Jesus is Lord and the Holy Spirit enters the heart of the believer, we find the empty places filled, and the dark sides of our soul transformed. We are in the process of becoming "new creatures in Christ." My personal experience is that a relationship with Jesus Christ changes everything in our lives; it makes all of life more rewarding, joy-filled and hope-full.

Why do people need Christ? Because without him we will always be lost and our lives will never realize their God-given potential. He opens the door to a whole new world for us. He enriches every life he touches. He changes the world one person at a time, as his kingdom expands across the globe.

This leads to the second question with which I wrestled:

Why Do People Need the Church?

Why do people need the Church? I have intentionally capitalized Church for I am here speaking of not one specific church but the idea of church—a gathering of Christians who worship, serve, and grow together. It is important to ask this question for there are many in our society who would say that they "believe in" Jesus, they simply do not see the need for "organized religion." They say that they can worship "in my own way" without being connected to a church. In a world where such views are so prevalent, pastors and church leaders must have a fundamental conviction about the absolute necessity of the Church if they are going to lead the Church.

Here are several answers that I find helpful. First, Jesus founded the Church! He organized his followers, promised to build a church upon the faith and witness of Peter and the other apostles, and sent the Holy Spirit to empower this fledgling organization. Jesus must have felt the Church was important to his work. In the New Testament the Church is even called Christ's "bride"! There are a host of reasons why the Church is not optional, but an absolutely essential part of God's plans for the world, and for each individual believer. We'll recount just six of them here.

1. The Church As the Continuing Incarnation of Jesus in the World

The apostle Paul writes that the Church is the "body of Christ." It is the incarnation of Jesus in the world today; it is charged with doing what Jesus did, speaking on behalf of Jesus, being his hands and voice. The Church is the vehicle of God's saving and transforming work in the world.

2. The Church Is the Temple of the Holy Spirit

The Church is the temple of the Holy Spirit. Paul and Jesus both make clear that Christ is uniquely present where believers gather together. Jesus said, "where two or three are gathered in my name, I am there among them." It was when the believers were gathered together and praying with one another that the Holy Spirit descended upon them.

3. The Bible Commands Us to Meet Together to Encourage One Another

The Bible specifically commands believers to gather together. Listen to the words of Hebrews 10:24-25, "And let us consider how to provoke one another to love and good deeds, not neglecting to meet together, as is the habit of some, but encouraging one another, and all the more as you see the Day approaching." The entire New Testament presupposes that Christians will live out their faith in community. The New Testament was written, nearly entirely, to churches. And there would be no Christianity today were it not for the fact that believers gathered together for the last two thousand years.

4. Christians Can Accomplish Far More Together Than They Can Apart

The work of Christ can never reach its true potential when individual Christians try to go it alone. Imagine the difference in impact and power of one solo Christian trying to follow Christ and change the world, worshiping, doing evangelism, and developing his or her own mission work versus an entire group of people using their combined resources and sharing their common gifts for ministry with one another. Furthermore, the Church helps turn the good intentions of individuals into action.

5. Each Believer Is Gifted by the Holy Spirit for Work in the Church

The Bible teaches that each Christian is given certain gifts or abilities by the Holy Spirit when one becomes a Christian. These gifts are not given for our own edification, but to help strengthen others. Part of being a Christian includes using the gifts God has given each of us to build up others in the Church.

6. The Church Is Essential for Becoming a Deeply Committed Christian

No one will ever realize full potential as a Christian apart from the Church. It is in worship, fellowship, discipleship, and service that we grow and become the people God longs for us to be, and each of these means of growing in Christ is best accomplished within the context of the Church.

Just as people need Christ, they also need the Church; it is not optional, but absolutely essential to God's plan for our lives. Being a part of a healthy congregation is a source of great joy and the means for great growth and ministry in the life of a believer.

After I had answered these two questions in the summer of 1990 as I prepared to launch a new congregation, there was one last question that had to be answered.

Why Do People Need *This Particular* Church?

This was a very important question, for there were nearly twenty other churches already in existence in the community in which we were launching. Why start one more? To answer this question I had to be clear about the theological and spiritual distinctiveness of my own denominational heritage. What is unique or different about United Methodism that would prove helpful to some in this community? How might we be uniquely equipped to reach those who didn't attend church? What unique gifts did I have as pastor that might help us reach people not currently being reached? What would we like to be known for? What was the distinctive calling Christ had given us?

These questions are increasingly important for any church to answer in today's world. It is no longer viable for a denominational church to open its doors and assume that all of the people of that denomination in the community are going to attend. The only church where this still works, and even then only in a diminished way, is the Roman Catholic Church, where "brand loyalty" is still very high.

It might be helpful if we examine this last question from a business perspective. If you decided to open a bookstore in your town, knowing that there were ten other bookstores within driving distance, what would you do? You would have to make sure that your bookstore offered something the others did not. You would have to excel at either selection, location, service, atmosphere, price, or perhaps you would focus on a particular genre of books: children's, or used books, or trade books. Finally you might offer features the other bookstores did not offer—perhaps a café, or music, or a children's play area. But if you simply offer another bookstore that looks like all of the others, your bookstore stands little chance of succeeding.

> **Each congregation, regardless of how small or how large its membership, must strive to excel in some area.**

Each local congregation must do the same thing. Regardless of how small or large its membership, each must strive to excel in some area. Large churches should excel by offering large numbers of options and quality that will be difficult to replicate across the board in the small church. Small churches can offer intimacy, outstanding pastoral care with a personal relationship with the pastor, excellent follow-up on visitors (whose names should be remembered by the pastor when they visit a second time), and personal attention in Sunday school. The small church may focus on one or two ministries that it does extremely well. And it will likely have an advantage in location for those living near them. An additional advantage is that many people prefer a small-church feel, so long as the church services are done with quality—the preaching is good, the music is good, and the fellowship is genuine and excellent. The upside potential for a large church is the large number of options it can offer in worship times, ministries and programs, and the quality with which it can offer these programs. Regardless of a church's size, each should choose to excel at certain things that its congregation members can be proud of, and that are attractive to newcomers or the unchurched in the community.

I often ask this question of pastors I meet: Assume for a moment I live in your neighborhood. Now tell me why should I attend the church that you serve? I get all kinds of interesting answers. But what I am looking for is an utter conviction that the pastor or church leader believes that her or his church is the "best thing since sliced bread." I want to see a passion in that person's eyes, hear a conviction in the tone of voice and observe an excitement in the body language when each talks about her or his church.

When you have compelling answers to these questions, when you truly believe that people need Christ, that the Church is essential to God's plans in helping people develop fully into Christian disciples, and that the church you serve has wonderful things to offer, you are ready to lead your church to change the world!

If I were to ask the leaders in your church these three questions, what would they say?

THREE

The Fourth Question

I've discussed the burning questions that must be answered in order to develop a highly effective church. However, there is one last question that must be answered by each pastor, church leader, and congregation:

To Whom Does Our Church Belong?

To whom does our church belong? Until the appropriate answer is given to this question, the church will always struggle. And this is one of those questions that truly has only one correct answer. But I'll begin with the wrong answers.

The church does not belong to the denomination, the bishop, or the denominational hierarchy, even if each has a "trust clause" in the church's legal deeds stating the contrary. The church does not belong to the pastor, even if he or she was the founding pastor. The church does not belong to the choir director or any other staff member, even if these people have been in leadership for decades. The church does not belong to the lay leadership, the board, or any other official group in the church—not even the trustees. And no, the church does not belong to the members, though without them it would cease to exist. *The church belongs to Jesus Christ.* He is its Lord. He is its owner. The church is Christ's body, his representative to the world; a world for which he died.

The practical implication of this insight is profound. *The driving mission of every local church must be to do the things that Jesus wants us to do*—nothing less. But how do we know what Jesus wants us to do with his church? We can discern what he would have us do today by looking at what he actually did when he walked on earth. Jesus said that his driving passion was to "seek out and to save the lost" (Luke 19:10). Jesus spent a large part of his time with "sinners" seeking to bring them back to God. He even included this in his Great Commission. If this was Jesus' driving passion, it must be our driving passion in our churches.

Jesus' ministry included healing broken minds, bodies, and souls. For today's church this means excellent pastoral care, not only for those within the membership of the church, but for those outside the church. Jesus' healing ministry was a demonstration of God's love, grace, and power to those who were outside of the synagogue as well as to those within. His ministry included teaching and preaching the good news of the Kingdom—something done both formally, in the synagogue or temple, and informally, in the streets and in the homes of people. Today this is Bible study, effective preaching, small groups, home groups, and for some, ministry on the airwaves. Jesus' ministry included preaching and teaching about ethical matters, while demonstrating care for the hungry and those in need. This is the prophetic work of the church, and its compassion and justice ministries. Each of these would be a part of faithfully continuing the ministry Jesus pursued as he walked this earth.

> Jesus said that his driving passion was to "seek out and to save the lost." If this was Jesus' driving passion, it must be our driving passion in our churches.

Another implication of the truth that our churches belong to Jesus Christ is that everything you do as a church and as a church leader must be surrounded in prayer. Your highest aim is to know and do Christ's will. Prayer is an essential part of discerning the will of God. Before every church meeting our leaders pray, seeking God's will. Before every major decision is made we are on our knees. Everything in the church should be aimed at doing Christ's will. While the church may not always agree as to what the will of Christ is, being clear that this is the central aim goes a long way in allowing a church to make important and difficult decisions.

At Church of the Resurrection we have sought to be guided by this principle from the very beginning. When we outgrew one worship service in the small chapel we rented, we raised the idea of starting a second worship service. Initially our members did not want to do this, "because we won't know everyone anymore." But when we asked the question, "What did Jesus put us here for? What does he want from us? What was his driving passion?" We remembered that Jesus' driving passion was reaching lost people. Now we asked the question again, "In light of Jesus' driving passion of reaching lost people, which would seem to be Christ's will for us, his church: to maintain one worship service where there is no longer room to receive anymore lost people, or to expand to two worship services to make room for all?" Putting the question in these terms, and remembering that our aim was not to do what we wanted, but what Christ wanted, and then recalling the things that were most important to Christ, helped us quickly and easily make hard decisions.

This continues to be true. We have had literally hundreds of decisions like this. Every ministry area in the church is charged with applying this type of logic and these basic principles to the decisions they make.

One of the most helpful books on this subject, and one that most pastors I know wish they had written, is Rick Warren's, *The Purpose-Driven Church* (Zondervan, 1995). The principles he articulates in this book are so simple, and yet capture the essence of effective church leadership. Warren's text should be required reading in every seminary and every local church.

In leading your church, remember who the church belongs to. Your driving mission should be to please Christ and to do the things that he would have you do. The pastor's job is not first to determine what the laity want to do, and then do it. Nor is it to determine what the denominational leaders want done. Neither is it simply to pursue your own visions for ministry. Instead, you are called to seek Christ's will for his church. If you fail in this you will have missed the very purpose of the church!

Is your congregation's driving passion to do what Christ wants to do? Does it believe that the church belongs to Christ above all? If so, then perhaps the congregation is ready to get the word out, by marketing the church.

FOUR

Marketing the Church

There has been something of a disagreement in the church world in the last twenty years about the merits of using marketing strategies in the church. Some believe this taints the church, while others unabashedly steal from Madison Avenue.

It is interesting that in the last few decades corporate America has recognized the connection between marketing and evangelism. In the 1980s Apple Computer hired a select group of outstanding sales representatives and called them "Macintosh Evangelists"! These people were absolutely persuaded that every man, woman, and child needed a Macintosh computer. They believed, with everything that was within them, that the Apple Macintosh was a superior product in every way to the other platforms of home computers. Their job was to persuade the world of their convictions.

Let me be clear about the definition of marketing that I am using. Merriam-Webster's Collegiate Dictionary, tenth edition, tells us that marketing is the act of selling. Selling has a host of definitions, among which is the following:

"5 a : to develop a belief in the truth, value, or desirability of : gain acceptance for b : to persuade or influence to a course of action or to the acceptance of something [as a doctrine, belief, or activity]"

Marketing, as it relates to the church, is the effort made to persuade others of their need for what your church offers while explaining the ways your church will meet this need, and doing so in a way that inspires and motivates them to respond.

In a sense, every time a Christian seeks to persuade a non-Christian to come to church or when a pastor seeks to persuade the congregation to follow Christ—they are marketing. They are trying to help another see why this person needs what is being offered and seeking to motivate and inspire them to respond. Every sermon I preach is a sales presentation of sorts; I am hoping to persuade the congregation members of the benefit of living out the implications of the scripture passages I am preaching from. And, to the degree that some actually do it, I have "closed the sale."

> **Market research should also include future trends: information about the number of new households that will be expected in the area and any changes in the existing community. This information is invaluable.**

Marketing has been essential to Church of the Resurrection. When we first began we had no building, no land, no programs, only a dream. Our challenge was to get the word out about our dream, to let people know we were in existence, and to invite and motivate the unchurched to come for a visit. What follows is a bit of what worked for us.

First, most of us are aware of what is commonly called, "market research." In the case of a local church, this involves the science of studying the community surrounding the church: understanding the people that are there, how they think, what their perceived needs are, what the makeup of the average household looks like. This study should also include future trends: information about the number of new households that will be expected in the area and any changes in the existing community. This information is invaluable. It is used to help the church plan for the future, as well as to guide the church's ministry in the present.

In 1996, when hundreds of new apartments began to spring up in our community, we asked, "Who will be moving into these apartments?" In our community the answer is typically professional single persons over thirty years of age. What was clear during construction was that there would be nearly one thousand new singles moving into the area within five minutes of our church. Market research shows that a large number of single persons are not actively involved in a local church, often reporting that they feel that the church is only for married couples. Yet one of the tremendous needs of singles is for community.

This market data identified an underserved part of the population that would include many nonreligious and nominally religious people. We determined that if we were to be faithful to our mission, we must try to reach this group and that we must strive to be a church that clearly cared about and valued singles.

We did not change our message, but we did change some of our language. We tried to be sensitive in how we spoke about people, such as not always using the term *family* as though it included only married couples. We highlighted the fact that many of our staff were single. We sought to make sure that singles were represented in leadership in the church. We looked to have singles as ushers, greeters, and in other visible capacities. We then developed a vision for a singles program based upon the felt needs of our single members and staff. We hired staff members who could implement these programs and we designed a brochure aimed at attracting the attention of singles, which articulated the reasons why they should attend our program, and what needs they had that would be met by our new singles ministry. The brochure sought to communicate the church's welcome and desire to be a church for singles. We then sent out our brochure as a direct mailing to all of the apartment buildings within a five-mile radius of the church. The result was that more than two hundred singles attended the opening night of our new singles program and today more than eight hundred are a part of our constituency.

As I mentioned, marketing was critical to our fledgling new church when we began in 1990. We had no building and no sign during the week. We were an invisible church until Sunday mornings when we would erect a real estate sign in front of our rented chapel. No one would have known that we existed if we had not advertised. And so we relied heavily upon various forms of marketing all aimed at telling our story, inviting people to worship, and bringing people in the doors of the church.

Here's what worked for us in the early years. To get a database of potential members (marketers would call these "leads") we utilized a telemarketing campaign. We set up a phone bank with ten telephone lines in the basement of another church and recruited members of two existing United Methodist churches to help us call six thousand households in one week. We had a script outlined for each caller. We utilized information from a crisscross directory that we had purchased. (A crisscross directory is a phone book arranged by street address, allowing callers to select a geographic area to make their calls.) Each caller could make one hundred phone calls in the hour and a half they were with us each day. With ten phone lines working at the same time we made six thousand calls in six days. In each call we asked if these persons were currently involved in another church. If they were not actively involved in another church we asked if we could send them more information about our new church. Six hundred people we called indicated that they were unchurched and that they would be willing to receive more information. The power of this marketing method comes from the fact that we now had the names of six hundred households (about eighteen hundred people) in which the people described themselves as unchurched! Almost all of our charter members came as a result of this telemarketing campaign, about sixty households in all.

As our callers made notes about each prospect, they would sometimes write that one was a particular "hot prospect," meaning that he or she seemed quite eager for more information. In the weeks that followed the calling campaign, I followed up with a personal telephone call and an in-home visit to those who would allow me to come by. These that I visited in their homes often became the leaders of our church.

When we finally held our first worship service we had about one hundred twenty prospective members from the community in attendance. Nearly all of these came from either the direct mail or telemarketing campaigns.

Following the telemarketing campaign, we sent out three direct mail brochures to the entire community, mailing to ten thousand households each time, including those we had contacted by phone. These brochures announced the grand opening of our church and described our vision. They were aimed at attracting the attention of the unchurched rather than trying to lure members from other congregations. In addition to these pieces, we mailed a personalized letter and a hand-addressed invitation to our first worship service to those who responded to the telemarketing campaign.

When we finally held our first worship service, about six weeks after the telephone campaign, we had about one hundred twenty prospective members from the community in attendance. Nearly all of these came from either the direct mail or telemarketing campaigns.

Over the next four years we continued to rely heavily upon direct mail to help us get the word out about our church. We also utilized Yellow Pages advertising and newspaper advertising, but neither of these had the impact that direct mail had in helping us reach new people.

We typically sent three direct mail pieces per year. Unchurched people naturally consider attending church at Christmas and Easter, so we targeted most of our mailings to these two times. These two mailings were always very successful. A third mailing was usually done in the summer as the schools were starting back up.

Sending out ten thousand two- or three-color brochures cost approximately two thousand dollars. We knew that if even three households joined the church as a result of the mailing, it would pay for itself in the first seven months. But these members would be attending and contributing for far more than seven months. Furthermore, each of these members would likely invite another friend or neighbor to the church in the next year.

Direct mailings became more and more effective the longer we continued using them. Many people would respond only after receiving our mailings for two or three years. At our peak we had two hundred households visit the church from one direct mail piece we sent out advertising the grand opening of our new building and our candlelight Christmas Eve services.

Another way that we utilized our direct mail brochures was having enough extra printed so that we could give two or three to each worshiper the weekend before Christmas Eve or Easter.

We would then ask our member to pray for a neighbor, coworker, or family member who did not go to church, and then hand deliver the brochure to this person, inviting her to worship. The brochure, the prayer, and the personal invitation were a very successful combination in persuading people to visit. An added benefit of the direct mailings is that they made our own church members feel very proud of their congregation; it built up the congregation's own self-esteem and created a public image of our congregation that made it easier for members to invite their friends.

Marketing comes in other forms, of course, including signs (most existing churches underutilize their signage potential), radio, television, and more. In our setting, direct mail has been our most successful form of paid advertising.

How has your church intentionally sought to reach out to unchurched people? In what ways do you communicate to your community?

One last bit of advice about direct mail: Do it well, do it positively, do it regularly, and send it to thousands of households. Doing it well means that the quality, the concept, the artwork, the paper, and colors should all be sharp. A poorly designed mailer can do more harm than good. I suggest having the pastor and one or two talented graphics or marketing people design the piece. It should not be designed or tweaked by committee. The piece will lose its edge and effectiveness if too many people are a part of the design process. Doing it positively means that your message should be a positive one; negative messages tend to turn unchurched people away (though the people in your church may like them). Doing it regularly means sending out mailings two or three times per year for several years. Direct mailing has a residual effect; many respond only after the fourth, fifth, or sixth mailing they receive. Finally, direct mail works on the "law of large numbers." Your response rate for a well-designed direct mail piece might be only one-tenth of one percent; if you send out three thousand pieces that might indicate that as few as three to as many as ten households would visit. Often the response rate is much higher, but be prepared for a rate within this range. It is also less expensive, on a per-piece basis, to mail to five thousand households than it is to mail to one thousand.

Several advertising agencies specializing in churches can help you with your design work. Among these are Outreach Marketing, Inc. (*www.outreachmarketing.com/outreach*), Details Communications (*www.detailscom.com*), and the Church Ad Project (*www.churchad.com*).

I will conclude with one final story to illustrate the importance of marketing. Several years ago I was invited to an event at a United Methodist church in a neighboring town. I failed to take the address of the church with me, but I wasn't worried since the church was a long-established church in a town of only a few thousand people. I was certain that I could find it. When I arrived in the town I stopped by the gas station and asked if anyone knew where this church was. Not a soul knew of the church. I stopped by the local convenience store. Eight people were inside when I asked aloud, "Does anyone know where the United Methodist church is?" No one knew. It wasn't until I stopped an elderly couple walking down the street that I discovered that I had been within two blocks of the church the entire time. But no one in the gas station or convenience store had heard of this congregation. Though they had likely driven by its building many times, the church had become invisible. People no longer noticed it; it blended into the landscape. What church members needed to do was let the community know they were there, that they were alive, that they wanted to be of service, that they offered something of vital importance, and that all were welcome. This church could have benefited from marketing.

How has your church intentionally sought to reach out to unchurched people? In what ways do you communicate to your community? How might you utilize the above information in your congregation? Once you've begun to plan for marketing your church, your next task will be to analyze the first impressions visitors will form about your church.

FIVE

The Little Things

Leaders recognize that the little things play a key role in the success or failure of any organization. This is never more true than in the church. First-time visitors, as well as members, often notice the little things. First-time visitors may form a negative impression of the kind of church you are, and may never have an opportunity to see your strengths if you have not paid attention to the "little things." For your members, the little things will play an important role in shaping your church's entire culture and how members pursue ministry. Let me give a couple of concrete examples.

Several years ago I was invited to tour the facilities of a nearby United Methodist church. The first thing I noticed as I got out of my car was that the grass hadn't been mowed recently. This stood out in a community where the homes had perfectly manicured yards. As I approached the doors I encountered the church's trash bags, left by the front door.

> **Most visitors in worship do not wish to be recognized, but they do want others to be friendly and welcoming.**

One had been torn open by a dog and had trash strewed around it. As I entered the foyer, I noticed that there were missions donations everywhere, which would have been very exciting if only they had been organized in some way and stacked. As it was, the foyer simply looked cluttered. The pastor met me and was excited to take me to the sanctuary. I said, "Before taking me to your sanctuary, take me to your nursery." The nursery had no windows. The ceiling tiles were stained with water from a leaky roof and were bowed down and looked like they could break. A quick glance at the toys yielded play typewriters with broken keys, a doll without a head, and a host of toys that looked like they needed to be retired. But what I noticed most about the nursery was the smell—a cross between mildew and dirty diapers with a hint of

Lysol. This was a first impression that even the best preaching and music would not overcome for a parent of a small child.

A first-time visitor begins formulating her feelings about your congregation before getting out of the car. These first impressions are formed by the appearance of your facilities and grounds, the quality of your signage, and the congestion of your parking lot. At Church of the Resurrection, our facilities staff is asked to look at the building and grounds from the view of a first-time visitor. Does the condition of our facilities honor God? Does it say that we believe what we are doing here is important? Does it demonstrate quality and caring?

We ask that our mowing crews come on Thursday or Friday each week during the warmer months so that the grass looks kept when visitors arrive on Sunday. As I am walking in from the parking lot I look around for trash and pick it up. If the trash bin doors are open on Sunday morning as I am coming into the church, I will close them. I am neither above picking up trash nor willing to walk past it and hope someone else picks it up.

Exterior and interior signage is also very important. We've got some work to do on this at Church of the Resurrection. Here I mean both monument signs that will guide first-time visitors to specially marked first-time visitor parking near the door you wish them to enter, and interior signage that will clearly guide a first-time visitor everywhere he needs to go. By having a special parking area reserved for first-time visitors, you can strategically place parking lot greeters in this area, and you can control which entrance most first-time visitors will enter, allowing you to set up a special information station at that entrance. It is advisable to evaluate your facilities from time to time from the perspective of a first-time visitor. Is your narthex and entry appealing or is it filled with clutter? Do your bathrooms appear neat and clean? Are there ceiling tiles that have water stains, or potholes in the parking lot? Do you have a clearly marked information center? Are the paint, carpet, and walls in good condition? Has the building been updated in the last five to ten years? Is it well lit and cheerful?

For those with infants and toddlers the most important room in the building, as I have noted, is the nursery. Do your nurseries look bright and cheerful? Do your nursery workers appear professional and loving? Does your process for taking children into the nursery inspire confidence on the part of the parents? Do you have a way for the nursery workers to contact the parents in the event of an emergency?

Other elements of making a good first impression include caring greeters at every entrance to the building *and* in each of the Sunday school departments. Within the context of worship we invite members of the congregation to stand and greet one another at the beginning of each worship service. At the same time we are careful not to make the first-time visitors stand out; most visitors in worship do not wish to be recognized, but they do want others to be friendly and welcoming. I'll talk more about how to get to know your first-time visitors in the next chapter.

When it comes to the beginning of worship, note that whoever speaks first will set the emotional and spiritual tone of the service. Do not ask a low-energy person to give the words of welcome and greeting unless you would like a low-energy service. I begin each worship service with a very high-energy greeting, and follow that by introducing myself. I begin worship each week with these words, "Good morning! Welcome to the United Methodist Church of the Resurrection! We are so excited that you are here today! My name is Adam Hamilton. I am the senior pastor and we are so grateful that you have chosen to worship with us today!" This introduction of the worship leader or pastor by name is important. I have visited more than one hundred churches and I usually have no idea who is speaking to me and leading the worship service until we get to the sermon—at which point I look in the bulletin and usually find a name next to the sermon title. I then look at the list of staff people to see if the person preaching is indeed the lead pastor. Until then I didn't know if the worship leader was the pastor, the associate pastor, or a layperson. This is one more detail that leaves the first-time visitor feeling like an outsider. But when the pastor or worship leader introduces himself it creates the feeling that visitors were expected and are welcome.

It would take an entire book to describe the host of different details and little things that can sabotage or enhance a church's effectiveness at fulfilling its mission. Great leaders notice these details and have an eye for the little things. They are constantly striving to see their activities through the eyes of their "customers" and are aiming for continuous improvement.

Several examples from the fast-food industry might help you think through what this means in your local church. I stopped by a fast-food restaurant not long ago. The closing mechanism on the door was broken, which resulted in the door slamming shut loudly every time a customer walked in. Throughout my lunch I watched as diners flinched every time the door slammed. While the food was fast, hot, and prepared with quality, this is not what stood out during my dining experience. What stood out was the door slamming. Likewise, looking at trash cans that are overstuffed or bathrooms that are not well kept or tables that have not been cleaned or even seeing employees behind the register whose shirts are wrinkled or dirty all create impressions about the restaurant that might cause a customer to reconsider a second visit. Leaders, whether they are fast-food restaurant managers, local church pastors, or staff or committee chairs, are responsible for making sure that attention is paid to the details, so that even in the little things the church is creating an environment that supports what you hope are positive first impressions for your visitors, while developing a culture of excellence among your existing members and staff.

What are the first impressions your visitors would form of your church? Are there areas that need improvement? Who will champion the effort to improve quality in these areas?

SIX

Effective Follow-up Strategies

Having considered marketing strategies to invite people to church, and paying attention to the details so that your building, people, and programs work together to create positive first impressions for those who visit, in this chapter I invite you to consider effective follow-up strategies for first-time visitors.

Nearly every church, even in the most depressed setting, will have an occasional first-time visitor. Many churches will have four or five first-time visitors a month; some will have that many in a week. Every time a first-time visitor walks in the doors of your church an opportunity unfolds. This individual or family has taken the time to worship with you for some reason. Visitors likely have a need they are wondering if you can fulfill. If these persons had their own home churches, they would likely not be visiting, so the chances are that each visitor is one of the nonreligious that Jesus came to reach. The question is, What kind of follow-up will you do to encourage each one to come back?

One pastor I know is quite proud of the fact that his church does nothing to follow up on first-time visitors. He believes that to do so will somehow taint the church's mission. He said that he is proud of this fact because it indicates that the only people who joined the church were those who *really* wanted to, who had taken their own initiative to do so. But I feel he misses the point. He assumed that visitors were generally Christians who, if they did not join his church, would join another. But this can no longer be assumed in a post-Christian era.

At Church of the Resurrection we look at every first-time visitor as someone who may be genuinely unchurched, for whom this may have been the first time in years that he decided to visit a church. It may have taken a great deal of courage, or a great need, that prompted him to come. Often visitors come only after a friend has invited them five or six times. If this is the case, we want to do everything in our power to help the visitor feel the welcome of Christ through our church and to motivate him to want to return the following week.

Last year I joined the health center at the local community college. I received the orientation to the equipment, had my photo ID made, got dressed in my gym clothes and worked out. I had a good experience, I felt better afterward, I enjoyed being there and I planned to go back two to three times a week from that time forward. That was ten months ago, and I have yet to go back. I need to work out, I enjoyed working

> **Effective follow-up is designed to offer encouragement and motivation for the visitor to choose to return for a second, or third, or fourth visit.**

out, but I struggle in making the time and taking the initiative to return. This is where many of our first-time visitors find themselves after they visit our worship. If they have a great experience they likely will want to come back. They may believe it is important. They may recognize that they, or their children, need it. But they must combat the spiritual and psychological inertia that creates something of a mental block when they think of returning the next week.

Effective follow-up is designed to offer encouragement and motivation for the visitor to choose to return for a second, or third, or fourth visit. This is among the most important things a pastor or leader will do if she is seriously interested in reaching the unchurched and revitalizing the congregation.

From the time I began Church of the Resurrection, I believed my most important responsibilities were to (1) articulate a vision for the church, (2) preach the highest quality sermons I could preach, and (3) follow up on every first-time visitor within thirty-six hours of his or her visit to the church. I am convinced that the last of these—following up on first-time visitors—played one of the most critical roles of all in the success of our congregation. Let's take a look at the different types of follow-up processes we used in the early years of our church.

Get the Name and Address of First-Time Visitors

In order to have effective follow-up with first-time visitors, you must acquire the person's name, address, and phone number. We have found that the most effective way to get this information is through the use of attendance notebooks. Our notebooks are custom designed and based loosely upon a model I had seen in *Net Results* years ago. The notepads have a pocket on the left-hand side to hold our newsletter and other information about the church for our first-time visitors. The right-hand side contains our registration pads with one side reserved for members, the other side for visitors.

We do not place these at the end of the aisle and leave to chance whether they get passed during the service; too often they would not get passed. Instead, we stop in the middle of the worship service and I invite the ushers to come forward and distribute the notebooks in the same way that the offering plates are distributed. I then state, "We would be grateful if you would sign in and let us know that you were here this morning. If you are a first-time visitor, please feel free to take the information on the left-hand side of the notebook. After you have signed in, please pass the notebook down the aisle. *Be sure to take a look and see who is sitting next to you and where that person lives; there may be someone who lives in your neighborhood sitting right next to you. Be sure to greet those sitting next to you by name after the service of worship.*" With this last line of instruction we make it difficult for a visitor not to sign in and leave his address. A visitor may be reluctant to give you this information, but since the pastor has just asked the congregation members to look at the names and addresses of those sitting next to them, the visitor feels compelled to comply. The vast majority of people who visit our church sign in.

Getting "Mugged" at Church of the Resurrection

The following steps were done exactly in this way until we began to average more than five hundred people per weekend in worship attendance. Later in this chapter I will examine the method for follow-up we adopted once we surpassed five hundred per weekend.

After worship each weekend I would tear off all of the attendance sheets and circle the names of first-time visitors. Following lunch with my family, I would take the attendance sheets, map out a route, and then begin following up with these visitors.

I have found that it is most effective to have something in your hand to give to your visitors when following up with them; the delivery of the gift becomes the reason for your visit. Some churches deliver fresh-baked cookies or bread as a gift of welcome. The downside with this gift is that the food will be eaten and leave no ongoing reminder of the church. Some give refrigerator magnets. But most people cannot tell you what logos appear on their refrigerator magnets. We found that coffee mugs were an effective gift, and one that is seldom discarded.

Our coffee mugs, printed with our logo, cost us between $1.50 and $2.50 each depending on the quantity, quality, and design. We order a new mug design and color each year. One innovative way that we helped pay for the mugs in the early years was to order twice as many mugs as we would need for the year. We then sold half of them to our members (who wanted to have the "new" mug to add to their collections) for twice what the mugs cost us. (We sold them for $3 to $5.) By doing this the mug sales paid for the entire program. Our members knew that by buying a mug (or a set of four) they would enable us to give a mug away for free to friends when they visited the church. (Mugs can be ordered through a local ad specialties company or through your local Cokesbury bookstore.)

Sunday afternoon, then, following lunch, I would take off, sometimes accompanied by one of my daughters, and I would begin delivering coffee mugs. I never called in advance for this visit. I just dropped by. Sometimes when a person came to the door she would look distressed to see the pastor on the doorstep, but I quickly assured the person that I did not want to come in. I would then say, "I just wanted to quickly drop this by and let you know how pleased we are that you visited the church this morning. I would love to have the privilege of being your pastor and we would love to be your church. This coffee mug is a small token of our welcome. And here is a copy of our newsletter. It will tell you more about the church. Do you have any questions?" Often the person had a question or two that I would answer, and then I would be off to the next visit. Once they knew that I would only stay a moment, that I was bearing a gift, and that I didn't need to be invited in, the visitors always relaxed and were usually amazed that the pastor stopped by to see them. I delivered more than eight hundred coffee mugs in four years and never once had a negative experience doing so.

> **Once they knew that I would only stay a moment, that I was bearing a gift, and that I didn't need to be invited in, the visitors always relaxed and were usually amazed that the pastor stopped by to see them.**

When the visitor was not home I would write a note on the newsletter expressing the same sentiments as above and then leave the mug near the garage door so the visitor would see it when she came in. An average visit lasted less than ten minutes. In the course of two hours I could easily deliver ten mugs. (During the first two years I averaged just three or four mugs a week, which I could deliver in less than an hour.)

Some have suggested that the laity should deliver these mugs instead of the pastor. In a larger church this becomes a necessity, to be sure. But in a smaller church, it is impossible to overstate the significance of the pastor delivering these mugs. Nearly every pastor I have told this to has dismissed it at first. But once they tried it, they found I was right; their retention rate of first-time visitors went up and they became more effective in connecting with and pastoring their flocks.

One of the other side benefits of this plan was that, because I had been to their homes, I tended to find it easy to remember the first-time visitors' names. So, when they visited again the second week, I would call them by name as they walked into the building. They were always amazed. But I could not have done this had I not delivered their coffee mugs. More than that, if I could call their names on the second visit, there was a strong likelihood that they would become members.

This investment of two to three hours a week, preferably on Sunday afternoon, but in no case later than Monday night, was among the most valuable uses of my time in developing the church. Our retention rate for first-time visitors was very high. In addition, I quickly came to know and build relationships with our visitors because I had stopped by their homes.

The Newsletter

After the mug visit we would make sure that each new visitor was added to our mailing list. Our newsletters have always been seen as evangelistic pieces. We try to ask, "How will new visitors feel about our church after reading this newsletter? Will it further motivate them to want to visit a second time?" We have a huge mailing list of all the people who have ever visited our church—more than ten thousand households representing nearly thirty thousand people. We view our mailing list and database as a valuable commodity. Most companies pay large sums to maintain lists of their prospective customers. We value this resource.

For our first six years in existence we mailed our newsletter every other week to everyone on our mailing list. Since we looked at each piece as an evangelistic piece, we felt that this served a valuable purpose. We often had people show up for a sermon or a special event who had visited a year before, and had not been back since. But they were still reading our newsletter from time to time. They saw something that interested them and it motivated them to come back.

As time went on and more households joined our mailing list, we began rethinking the types of mailings we used as well as the frequency with which we sent our mailings. Today, with so many households on our mailing list, we no longer mail every newsletter to all ten thousand households. Instead we mail full-color postcards announcing special events or sermon series that we believe the nonreligious or nominally religious might respond to (including postcards advertising our Easter and Christmas schedules) to all households on our mailing list. We may also mail one or two of our newsletters each year to everyone in our database. But our newsletter—sent now on a monthly basis—is customarily mailed only to members and regular or recent visitors. We have had a tremendous response to our postcard mailings, and they serve to encourage those who have visited in the past to worship with us again.

The In-Home Visit: Making a Pastoral Evangelism Call

During the first four years of our church's existence, until our average attendance passed five hundred per weekend, I would spend Monday evenings calling every visitor who had, the weekend before, attended the church for the third time. This required keeping track of all visitors and the number of visits they had made. Today we do that by computer, but at the time I did it using a recipe card file and three-by-five-inch cards upon which I recorded the name, address, phone number, and visit dates of each first-time visitor.

The purpose of my telephone call was to set up a time to come and visit in the homes of these prospective members. I have had many pastors tell me that prospects really don't want the pastor to come for a visit. But I have found that the key is all in how you ask. If a pastor calls a visitor and says, "Would you like me to come for a visit?" the answer will nearly always be "No." The visitor is a bit anxious about a visit from the pastor, or doesn't want to take the pastor's time. But when I spoke to a visitor and said, "Hello Jim, this is Adam from Church of the Resurrection. I am so excited that you and Jane have been worshiping with us! My goal is to get to know the people who worship at the church so I can be a better pastor to them and I would love to come by and get to know you and your family. Would that be okay?" In four years I never once had anyone turn me down for one of these visits. During that time I visited in the homes of more than five hundred people. Here's what happened on those visits.

I would schedule two to three visits a night, usually lasting no more than forty-five minutes each. Upon arriving at the home I would sit down with the individual or family and repeat the goal of my visit: to get to know them better, as well as to answer any questions they had about the church. I would then invite the prospective members to tell me their stories, such as where they grew up. If I was addressing a couple I would ask about how they met. I asked about their careers and how things were going in their lives. I asked about their church background. Dale Carnegie was right when he noted that people enjoy talking about themselves and they are grateful when someone listens and expresses an interest. After the family was finished sharing, I would tell them my own story, which included my testimony of how I came to faith in Christ and the difference Christ had made in my life. It was not "preachy" and did not feel like I was witnessing to them. It was just two or three people telling their stories. After I had shared my story I would share with them our vision for the church. I would outline for them the four expectations we have of our members. (More about that in the next chapter.) Finally, I would ask if I could pray for them.

Most unchurched people have never experienced having anyone pray aloud for them. Some experienced this as small children when parents or grandparents would pray with them, but have never experienced this as adults. Most of these had never had a pastor in their homes either. But because I was a pastor, my offer to pray with them seemed appropriate. We would join hands as we stood in the family room and I would pray for their children if they had any, or their job situation if they were between jobs. If they were married, I would pray for God to bless their marriage. And I would pray that God would guide them to the right church. If Church of the Resurrection was that church, I prayed for God to help them feel excited about the church; if not, that God would guide them to the right church

> During that forty-five-minute visit I had become their pastor and had shared the love of Christ with them.

for them. Often, when I finished praying, I would look up to see grown men and women with tears streaming down their faces. It was a very powerful time of ministry. And during that forty-five-minute visit I had become their pastor and had shared the love of Christ with them.

I can think of only one family, of the five hundred I visited in their homes, that did not ultimately join the church. When a pastor or church leader asks me to name the most important things that I did to help the church grow during our first four years, my answer is nearly always the mug and in-home visits.

Today, because of our size, it is no longer possible for me to visit in the home of every visitor. We have more than fifty first-time visitors each week. Now we have teams of laity who are our "muggers" and they deliver the mugs. They do a wonderful job. In addition I no longer go to the homes of each visitor after the third visit. Instead, we invite them to the church for Coffee with the Pastor, an hour-long session during which time I share with them my testimony and our expectations of members, as well as entertain questions. We have as many as 150 who attend this each month. Both of these programs grew as we grew, but I still maintain that if the church's size does not prohibit this personal involvement, the pastor should make it a priority to deliver mugs to first-time visitors and stop by the homes of the third-time visitors. This is still the most effective means of helping bring visitors to Christ.

Two final points about the importance of excellent follow-up. First, those in sales know that the best salespeople are those who develop a relationship with their potential customers, and who follow up with these prospects after an initial contact or a first sale. In the church, pastors, staff, and leaders are also in sales; we are trying to persuade people of their need for Christ and for the ministry of our church. What we are offering is *life*. We believe that our work is more than simply a matter of making a sale, or earning a commission. We believe God genuinely cares about our visitors, and that their lives would be radically changed for the better if only they would become followers of Jesus Christ. I can think of no greater motivator to inspire excellent follow-up. And second, the process I just outlined above is very similar to the follow-up processes I followed as a youth director in two churches while I was in college and seminary, with similar results. This section on follow-up is essential not only for pastors, but for program leaders, Sunday school teachers, and a host of others in the church. Follow-up is a critical key to success in any church ministry or program.

At Church of the Resurrection, I expect all of our program staff to develop outstanding and timely methods for providing follow-up to the first-time visitors in their ministry areas.

What does your church's follow-up process look like? What is your retention rate of first-time visitors?

SEVEN

Great Expectations

One of the common strands of information that emerged in the late-twentieth-century critique of mainline churches was that, by and large, they had "low expectations" of their members. We learned from Lyle Schaller that these churches expected little of their congregants and, as a result, their members performed according to these expectations. Worse than this, however, was the fact that organizations with low expectations are often perceived to be irrelevant or nonessential by their members. It becomes easy to drop out of such organizations.

United Methodist churches, like many mainline churches, have always asked members to support the church with their "prayers, presence, gifts, and service." But this was rather vague and innocuous. It wasn't always taken seriously when preparing people for membership. I recently heard from a "lifelong Methodist" who protested Church of the Resurrection's membership expectations and the requirement we had set stating that anyone joining a particular committee must actually fulfill these expectations. This longtime United Methodist said, "We've never had expectations before in The United Methodist Church!" That is the perception of many who joined our churches in the past.

In this chapter I will offer an alternative perspective on membership that differs from what is common in many of our churches, and I will examine ways that we, the ministry staff of Church of the Resurrection, have lowered the threshold to make it easy for people to join our church, while simultaneously raising the bar of expectations for membership. By means of these two seemingly opposing strategies we welcomed more than six thousand adult members and more than two thousand children in ten years, while seeing these persons move toward true discipleship as evidenced by their fulfillment of our expectations for membership.

What Is Membership?

I once knew an associate pastor of a church who told me that his primary task was to "get members." He would come back to the church after a visit with a prospective family and say, "I got two more members today!" This is indicative of an institutional mind-set that permeates many of our mainline churches stating that "membership is what counts." We learned from those above us in the hierarchy that the all-important number by which we would be evaluated was membership. When this becomes the measure of effectiveness or success in the ministry, pastors learn that "getting members" is our top priority.

> **When people join our church we have not clearly communicated expectations, we have not tried to share with them the essentials of the faith, or attempted to discern if they are truly on the road to discipleship.**

As a result we find that many mainline churches have done a passable job of listing names on the roster. But when people join our church we have not clearly communicated expectations, we have not tried to share with them the essentials of the faith, or attempted to discern if they are truly on the road to discipleship. We are just excited to get them to join. Consequently, we have membership roles that are often two to four times our actual average worship attendance. One Baptist church I visited had more than twenty thousand members, but an average worship attendance of five thousand! Many United Methodist churches are just as bad, with only one-fourth or one-third of members attending regularly.

One of the things I have appreciated about many of the Southern Baptist churches I have studied is that the most important figure they report is Sunday school attendance. Nearly every Baptist pastor I have met can tell you how many the church averages in Sunday school, while many can't tell you what the church's membership is. Attendance in a small group is a very good indicator of how effectively the church is discipling people.

On the opposite end of the spectrum from low-expectation churches who simply seek to gain "members" are a few very-high-expectation churches who see membership as a way of differentiating between the "real Christians" and everyone else. These churches are careful not to let anyone join until they are confident that these individuals' faith is genuine, and they are fully meeting all of the membership expectations. Many of these churches require a prospective member to be interviewed by a board of elders and have his or her membership request voted upon before being officially welcomed into the church. These churches are careful to make distinctions between members and nonmembers in their pictorial directories, their nametags, and even who can participate in the church's programs and activities. Congregations with this perspective on membership will often have a much smaller number of members than its average worship attendance.

It has been the trend, in recent years, in some mainline churches to require extensive membership classes before visitors can join the church. This effort has, in some ways, been a laudable attempt to try to take membership seriously. The goal is to teach about the church, its theology, its history, its expectations and requirements, and to help people make a genuine commitment to Christ and the church before they are welcomed as members. These classes may be as long as two years in some churches (mirroring the period of time sometimes used in the early church to prepare catechumens for baptism and full communicant status). In many they are twelve weeks; in some they are just two to four weeks.

Each of these different models begs the question, "What is membership?" In the institutional mind-set of the past, membership was a very important concept. But it is less clear today what membership really is, and what the biblical foundations of this idea are.

Jesus never spoke about membership. Neither did the apostles. When Jesus invited people to be his disciples he did not ask them to take a twelve-week membership class and then he would determine if they were fit to be members. He simply said, "Come and follow me." When Peter preached the first Christian sermon on the day of Pentecost his invitation was simple, yet profound: "Turn away from sin and toward Christ, and join us in the water where you can publicly identify with Jesus, commit your life to him, and receive his mercy and grace!" When several thousand people were baptized on the same day, as described in Acts 2:41, they simply responded to the invitation Peter had given them to come to Christ, and on that day they became a part of the church.

At Church of the Resurrection we view membership as a tool that we think best functions as a step toward true Christian commitment. For nonreligious and nominally religious people it signifies a growing desire to identify themselves as Christians and to express commitment to the church. We want to make it easy for persons to take this step, while clearly communicating that it is important and that membership comes with real expectations. Our only requirements are that persons attend our Coffee with the Pastor where they will learn of our membership expectations and then that they come forward at the conclusion of one of our worship services on joining weekend and accept their membership vows. Let me describe what happens at our Coffee and what our membership expectations are.

Coffee with the Pastor

Our Coffee with the Pastor is an idea that was shared with me by the Reverend Jeff Spillar from his work at Christ United Methodist Church in Mobile, Alabama. I called Jeff some years ago when we had so many people wanting to join the church that I could no longer personally visit them in their homes. People began coming forward to join the church on joining weekend without my having even met with them to communicate our expectations. Jeff said, "Adam, you've got to develop another system so that you can connect with all of these folks before they join." He suggested having coffee with them as a group before joining. That was the seed for our "Coffee with the Pastor" ministry.

When we first began doing this it was hard for me to accept. I still wanted to get to know each member personally and to visit in the person's home. There is no question in my mind that this is the most effective way of developing a church and helping persons to be effective members who are also growing as disciples. But clearly there was no returning to that model; we simply had more people than one or two pastors could keep up with. We contemplated sending laypeople on visitation teams but felt that for many nonreligious and nominally religious people such a visit would seem awkward, and might actually keep them from taking the next step toward joining. For visitors, as I noted in chapter 6, any in-home visit may seem threatening and might be something they would resist. In the cocooning culture in which we live people are no longer comfortable visiting with "strangers." A pastor has an entrée, because she or he is the pastor, and is seen and known through the weekly sermon. But a lay team may not be received in the same way. Some certainly will welcome them, but others will go so far as to drop out of church to avoid the experience of having "strangers" call upon them for a scheduled visit. Ultimately we decided that the idea of the Coffee gave us the best opportunity to offer a consistent message and to use my position as pastor as a kind of lure to draw some to the event.

When we began this ministry the Coffee was in my home. This allowed us to maintain a sense of intimacy for the event and enhanced the lure of the invitation for many who were honored by the prospect of being invited to the pastor's house (or who were just curious to see how our family lived). After a year the Coffee outgrew my home. (The last Coffee with the Pastor held at my home saw eighty people show up, with no where to put them all!) Today this event takes place at the church.

Coffee with the Pastor is held on the first weekend of the month, nine times per year. It is held on Sunday afternoons from 2:30 to 4:00 P.M. Joining weekend is the following weekend during worship. We offer plenty of childcare during the Coffees and anyone is welcome to attend. We send out invitations to those who we've identified as newcomers to the church and we advertise it in the newsletter, bulletins, and with signage throughout the building. We have a wonderful team of laypeople who handle the registration, welcome and greet attendees, provide refreshments, and act as hosts for the event.

As our visitors check in they receive an information packet about the church with brochures from the various ministry areas. As they enter the room they are able to help themselves to coffee or lemonade and cookies. The first thirty minutes of the Coffee include various staff members of the church describing key ministries and inviting persons to consider getting involved. These usually include children, youth, singles discipleship, and music ministries. Our director of evangelism will then share his story of how he first came to church as one who himself was nominally religious, and how he committed his life to Christ, was baptized, and began growing in his faith at Church of the Resurrection. Finally, at 3:00 P.M. I am invited to speak to the group (which currently averages about 150 people).

During the next forty-five minutes I share with them my story of how I came to faith in Christ and the way that Christ has transformed my life. I then tell them the church's story so that they can become a part of its history and begin to understand our culture and our vision. I share with them a bit of where we are going in the future. Finally, I share with them our membership expectations and the reasons for them (more on these below). We end with questions and then a prayer in which I pray for God's guidance for them to discern whether this is the church God would have them join. As we dismiss them they are invited to tour the facilities, or to stop by an adjacent room if they know they wish to join, so they can fill out the membership form and have a photograph taken. I always remain in the room and invite persons to stop by so I can meet them. I will usually spend the next forty-five minutes greeting people and hearing a bit of their stories. Most people who attend Coffee with the Pastor join the church.

The following weekend we invite those who are joining to come forward during the closing hymn of each worship service. We introduce them each by name to the congregation and then we ask them two basic questions for membership:

1. Do you wish to be a disciple and follower of Jesus Christ?
2. Will you make this your church family, allowing the people of this church to love and care for you, as together we serve God with our prayers, presence, gifts, and service?

Once the new members have responded as a group to these questions I turn to the congregation and say, "These persons have professed their faith in Jesus Christ and their desire to be a part of your church family. Will you welcome them, love them, encourage them, and be their church family?"

After the congregation has affirmed its willingness to do this, we greet our new members with applause, and then send them to the narthex where the congregation will come to greet them.

You will notice that we do not ask these persons to pledge loyalty to our denomination. This pledge is an anachronistic one that goes back to a time when people joined particular local churches because of the denominational affiliation. Most of our new members were not United Methodists in the past and are not ready to pledge loyalty to this denomination. Through my preaching and the church's teaching we aim to help our entire congregation come to appreciate our denominational heritage and to be proud of it. We want them to become life-long United Methodists. But the loyalty pledge to a denomination is difficult for those under forty to relate to or with integrity to accept.

> **We tell them that membership comes with only responsibilities and expectations. We tell them that membership, like marriage, is a sign of commitment.**

Membership Expectations

We tell our prospective members, at our Coffee, that membership is not required in order to participate in the life of our church. We let them know that they are welcome to visit for as long as they like. We make clear, up front, that unlike the American Express Card, membership in our church has no privileges, only expectations. We promise to visit them in the hospital, whether they are members or visitors. We will do their weddings and their funerals whether they are members or visitors. They may participate in any of our programs as a visitor. We'll even make up member nametags for visitors if they ask for one.

We tell them that membership comes with only responsibilities and expectations. If they join they are no longer able to park in the closer "visitor parking"! If they join they will receive the stewardship mailings in the fall, including a pledge card. If they join we will call upon them from time to time to ask for their help. We tell them that membership, like marriage, is a sign of commitment. Often people live together today before marrying, where they seem to have most of the benefits of marriage. Why do they marry then? Because the heart longs to express meaningful commitment. Membership is a commitment in which one expresses, "This is my church, I feel responsible for her. I am committed to her mission, vision, and ministry. I want to serve God here as I grow in my faith."

This conversation alone moves many of our visitors to want to become members; they want their membership to mean something. They want to become more committed to Christ and the church. The fact that membership is about responsibilities and expectations, not privileges and benefits, makes it all the more compelling.

Our ultimate goal as a church is to help persons become deeply committed Christians. As we developed our membership expectations in 1990 we asked this question, "What does it take to grow in Christ and to become a committed disciple of Jesus Christ?" At core I felt that if someone would worship regularly, commit to a small group or some other form of personal discipleship, would begin to serve God with his gifts, and would reorder personal priorities by moving toward tithing, this would be the basis for both growing in Christ, as well as helping the church accomplish its mission. These became our expectations. So now we ask that persons do not join the church until they are prepared to make the following commitments:

expectations ✗

1. Attend worship every weekend unless you are sick or out of town (members who travel out of town are encouraged to attend services in the location they are visiting).
2. Participate in at least one activity each year aimed at helping you grow in your faith apart from worship attendance (Sunday school, Bible study, reading the Bible at home, retreats or other short-term classes we offer).
3. Give of your time in Christian service at least once each year through the ministry of the church.
4. Give financially in proportion to your income with the goal of tithing.

These, of course, are simply restating the traditional membership vows to "support the church with your prayers, presence, gifts, and service." But in our expectation we have tried to focus not on the church's needs, but on the individual's needs as each seeks to grow in Christ. We have also tried to make these expectations a bit more specific and measurable than "prayers, presence, gifts, and service." While we have tried to make it relatively simple to fulfill these vows, allowing persons to agree to participate in only one activity or give of their time in only one area, our staff is focused on moving them beyond participating in just one thing, to seeing each member regularly involved in both small groups and Christian service.

We do measure our effectiveness in moving nonreligious people to become committed Christians by analyzing certain key indicators in light of the membership expectations. First we look at membership versus worship attendance. Worship attendance currently runs between 90 percent and 110 percent of membership on an average Sunday. We monitor our Sunday school, small-group and Bible study participation—currently about 45 percent of our membership including more than one thousand currently taking Disciple Bible Study, our most intensive study. We then survey members of our congregation from time to time to find out if they are using our weekly study guide with daily scripture readings (more about this in chapter 9). Currently 54 percent of those we survey report using the daily study guide readings in some way. We estimate that somewhere around 75 percent of our members will either be involved in a small group or use our study guides to help them pursue their own devotional life, or both during the course of the year. When it comes to our third expectation, we track all volunteer ministries in the church and then determine annually what percentage of our member households have actually given their time in Christian service during that year. The number is currently more than 80 percent. Finally, as it pertains to our last expectation for membership, we track our increase in giving each year over the prior year. If our members are actually moving toward tithing we would expect our giving to increase at a rate higher than our worship attendance growth, which is the case each year.

Every September we preach a series of sermons aimed at reminding our members of these expectations and inspiring and motivating them to take the next steps in growing in their faith and commitment to Christ. At this same time we have a "ministry fair" where tents are set up outside the church and the various ministries and small groups provide information and seek to recruit new members to their ministry. We have one Sunday in September with a mission focus during which we invite community and mission agencies to set up tables to recruit our members for service at their agencies. Finally, we have an emphasis during this month on our Adult Sunday school classes and other small groups aimed at inspiring members to grow deeper even as they commit to greater service in Christ.

It is important to reiterate that while we try to clearly communicate our expectations to our members before they join, once they are members it is the task of our staff and program areas to market their ministries in such a way that our new members are inspired to get involved. And it is my task, as senior pastor, to teach and preach in such a way that our members clearly understand the need for taking the next steps in involvement and commitment. Marketing at Church of the Resurrection is not simply something we use to invite people to church, but a tool every staff member must use to help our members see why their participation in a particular ministry or program will both help them grow in their faith and make a difference in the church and in the world.

Mountain Climbing at Church of the Resurrection

Various churches have different metaphors they use to map out the goal of the Christian life and to lay out a plan by which members can know how to move forward in their faith and commitment. The most popular of the current models is the baseball diamond that Rick Warren uses at Saddleback Church in southern California. It is simple and easy to understand. One begins at first base by joining the church; next, one progresses to second base by getting involved in growth groups; and one progresses ultimately toward home plate, in missions and service to the world. The primary drawback of this model is that it is linear in how it approaches growing in the Christian life. What we have found is that most people don't actually progress in the Christian life in this way.

We have many people whose first small-group activity at the church is joining a mission team serving low-income people in the inner city, long before they ever join the church. We have a number of people who take Disciple Bible Study, our most intensive Bible study, before joining the church. In fact, some make their decisions to follow Christ in this study that is really aimed at people who should be on second base in Saddleback's baseball diamond.

Recognizing this nonlinear way that people grow in Christ, we use mountain climbing as our metaphor. We have trail maps around the church and we speak of "scaling the spiritual summits." Our aim is to help people experience the mountaintops of discipleship, service, and mission to the world. Our goal isn't that our members merely climb a metaphorical mountain in these areas, but that they ultimately go back down to the valley to guide someone else to the summit.

I love this model because it recognizes several things. First, as I already noted, growing in Christ isn't a linear process. Some people begin their walk with Christ by serving on a mission to the poor, or through an in-depth Bible study, or through serving God with their time as an usher or choir member before they ever even join the church. Spiritual summits allow us to let people try out the various paths of discipleship in the order *they* choose. But it also recognizes that beginners are probably not ready for advanced trails. So we offer trail maps that allow a new Christian or even a seeker to find out what mission opportunities might be best for them, or which Bible studies or service areas might be within their grasp. We rate our trails, just like the National Park Service will rate the hiking trails, so that novice hikers don't get in trouble on an advanced trail, and so that advanced hikers can easily find the paths that will be most challenging for them.

One never exhausts all of the possibilities for growing and serving in Christ; Christianity provides an inexhaustible array of studies to explore and ministries to pursue.

I also love this model because it captures the depth of the Christian experience. Rather than feeling I have rounded home plate and have finished the task, the spiritual summits metaphor lets me know that there are always more paths to hike. No matter how many years I travel to Estes Park and hike at the Rocky Mountain National Park, I know I will never see all the beauty there is to see; there is always a new summit to explore. At the same time I never grow tired of walking the simple beginner trail and seeing Bear Lake with the view of the mountains reflected in its glassy waters. Similarly, one never exhausts all of the possibilities for growing and serving in Christ; Christianity provides an inexhaustible array of studies to explore and ministries to pursue.

What Is the Recipe for a Disciple?

Finally, it is important for both pastors and church leaders to have a clear view of the product we are aiming to produce in our churches. Jesus told us that we were to "go . . . and make disciples" (Matt. 28:19). If this is our goal, then we had better understand two things: What does the finished product look like? And what is the process for making one?

This question is of utmost importance to pastors and church leaders. I remember an old episode of the original television series *Star Trek* in which a small spaceship had crash-landed on an alien planet. All but a young girl were killed. The crew members' bodies were damaged beyond recognition. The child, too, was severely injured, but the aliens were able to save her life. In the process they tried to reconstruct her facial features. Unfortunately, they had never seen a human before, and thus they had no idea what one looked like. The results were most unfortunate. Likewise, when we as pastors and church leaders are unclear about what a disciple should look like, the results can sometimes be tragic.

What are the characteristics of a deeply committed disciple of Jesus Christ? At Church of the Resurrection we have borrowed from the preaching of John Wesley and others who summarized Jesus' great commandments by saying that Christians are those who love and serve God with their "head, their heart, and their hands."

To love God with our "head" is to have a solid understanding of what we believe and why. This includes reading the Bible informationally, knowing what it says. It includes loving God with our intellect. We believe Christians should be informed, thinking people. Ultimately being a Christian begins with a decision to accept Jesus as Lord and Savior.

To love and serve God with our heart is to cultivate a personal relationship with Jesus Christ. This is done through daily prayer, reading the Bible formationally, worship, and the openness to and desire for the Holy Spirit's work in our lives. John Wesley spoke of a "holiness of heart," or being "perfected in love," which was also a part of loving God.

Finally, loving God with our hands always translates also into loving our neighbors; it is using our time and talents in Christian service. This includes being involved with the needs of hurting people, giving away a portion of our resources to share with others, and ministering both within and outside of the church to demonstrate the love of Christ to others. Again, Wesley spoke of this as social holiness.

There are many other ways of talking about the committed Christian life; these are just three we use regularly at Church of the Resurrection. It is important to have some picture of what the committed Christian looks like, for without it, you cannot begin to chart out the steps it takes to build such Christians. But with a clear sense of the end you have in mind, you can begin designing the processes and ministries in your church that will help you produce such Christians.

What do you think a deeply committed disciple of Jesus Christ looks like? Are you on that path? Are your church members on the path? Do you have clear plans to help people grow in their faith? What are your church's membership expectations? Are they measurable and specific? When was the last time you lifted these expectations up to your people?

EIGHT

Reflections on "Traditional" Worship

Most of the first-time visitors to your church will come as "consumers." If they are considering becoming involved in a local church they will "shop" for a church the way they shop for a doctor, a grocery store, or a restaurant. For many unchurched and churched people alike the primary "product" they will be evaluating is the worship service.

While on vacation recently my family worshiped in a beautiful cathedral, the home of the largest mainline church in the city we were visiting. We were excited to experience a church tradition different from, but historically connected to, our own.

As the service began we looked to our bulletin for some direction, but the bulletin was confusing. With no introduction or welcome the service started right into a chant from the church's Book of Prayer. After finding the appropriate page, and attempting to pick up the rhythm of the chant, we finally gave up. Unable to participate, we read the words silently. The words were beautiful, but somewhat difficult to follow.

Next the worshipers around us pulled out the kneeler in our pew and began kneeling. We joined them, fumbling to find the next page in our Book of Prayer.

Soon we moved to a hymn. We found it in a hymnal despite having no cue, except for the actions of fellow worshipers, that we were switching books.

On the service went for an hour and a half. It concluded with the Eucharist. But even this sacrament was presented with no instruction as to whether all were welcome or how the church received the elements. My daughters—age eleven and fourteen—who have received the sacrament since they were quite small, were excited to go forward to receive, but whispered to me as we approached the altar, "Dad, what do we do here? How do they receive?" I asked the girls to follow my lead and we received the elements.

After the conclusion of the service we spent the next half hour talking about the experience. We all agreed that it was frustrating to worship with no direction on what to do and difficult to appreciate what we could not understand. One of my daughters noted, "Dad, we were not alone. Did you notice all of the other people who didn't seem to be paying attention? I don't think they got it either!"

Although I have served for many years as a pastor, have two degrees in Christian theology and ministry, and have studied church history, worship, and the liturgy, I was confused by that service. I was able to follow along, albeit with a bit of fumbling and frustration. But how would nonreligious or nominally religious persons—those who hadn't grown up going to church or who had limited church exposure growing up—experience a service like this? Would it speak to them? Would they have worshiped? Would they have felt compelled to return? My family's experience on that recent Sunday morning mirrors the experience of an entire generation of people who have tried mainline churches and turned away to find a church that is more accessible and less intimidating.

A great deal has been written about the changing expectations and needs of people regarding worship. Today's twenty-, thirty-, and forty-somethings are looking for worship that they can understand and in which they *experience* truth, worship, and God's presence. It is no longer adequate to design worship that is "theologically solid" as one pastor described her worship. Reading litanies and singing hymns that speak only to the intellect—and then only if one is paying very close attention—is not merely uninspiring to today's generation of unchurched (and even many of the churched); it is downright irritating.

One frustration of traditional worship is the way in which it moves—reminiscent of watching a young adult driving a car with a manual transmission for the first time, filled with jolts, poor transitions, a bit of engine revving, and occasional moments where the engine dies altogether. Most of our traditional worship services begin with an opening hymn. After we sing three verses, it's time to shift gears (with a bit of a jolt) to the next item on the agenda (often a prayer, creed, or liturgy). When that's over we shift gears again, nearly killing any flow that was beginning to develop when we fail to appropriately transition the litany or prayer to the anthem. The anthem may be good, but often the congregants cannot understand the words, or they are not adequately prepared to allow the anthem to be a vehicle for God to speak to them. Then we're on to the next gear.

> **Our aim is to offer worship that is, for our congregation, the perfect blend of scripture, tradition, experience, and reason.**

Many people enter the sanctuary on Sunday morning with their minds filled with a variety of thoughts. Some just had a fight with a spouse or children on the way to church. Some were running late. Others are preoccupied with what has happened in the last week. None are ready to jump right into worship. Most require at least one hymn just to get them in the spirit of worship. This is one reason why most contemporary services have three to six hymns or songs at the beginning of the service, designed to promote focus, spiritual centering, and genuine God-centered worship. Taking our time in helping move people in worship and developing smooth transitions that link each element of worship together are critical in offering excellent traditional or blended services.

I will be the first to admit that we still haven't completely figured this out at Church of the Resurrection. But our aim is to offer worship that is, for our congregation, the perfect blend of scripture, tradition, experience, and reason. I am convinced that these four ingredients, known as the Wesleyan Quadrilateral in Methodist circles, are the components of great worship. Let's take a look at each.

Four "Ingredients" of Worship

Scripture

I was visiting with a Roman Catholic priest one day when he said, "You know what really gets me about you Protestants? You talk a lot about the Bible and how important it is, but when it comes right down to it, we use more of the Bible in worship than you do! We read all of the Lectionary readings, we sing choruses taken directly from the scripture. And you Protestants read three or four verses from the Bible and call it good!" My friend may have overstated the case a bit, but in some ways he is correct. Our worship should be thoroughly biblical. This can happen, in part, when the entire service has as its common thread the scripture for the day.

At Church of the Resurrection we follow the announcements (which actually happen two minutes before worship officially begins) and the greeting with the theme for the day, taken from the biblical text. This theme will be found in most of the hymns, it will be incorporated into the pastoral prayer, it will be related to the anthem or special music before we ever get to the scripture that it is taken from. The sermon will then expound upon this theme, the offertory will be a response to it, the closing hymn will prepare the people to live the charge, and the benediction will drive the point home. All of these elements flow out of the scripture for the day.

My friend the priest mentioned one misconception that I find in some traditional Protestant worship as well: the idea that reading three scriptures or more in worship makes worship scriptural. When the average churchgoer, much less the nonreligious or nominally religious visitor, hears the scripture read, with little or no context given, it can be confusing and often does not speak to that person. It is not always an uplifting experience. It is often not an edifying experience. And even though the best lectionary preachers will try to tie each of the scriptures together, the sermon is divorced from the first scripture reading by as much as fifteen minutes. The average churchgoer is not getting it! And so we've taken our treasure and we've reinforced the idea that the scripture is mysterious, difficult to understand, boring, and irrelevant. Better to read one scripture and help people truly hear God speaking through it than simply to throw out three loosely connected lectionary readings with little or no transition or guidance in what to listen for. Or, if one is going to read all of the lectionary readings, then introduce each one and give some guidance to prepare people to hear and receive it.

As I'll note in a subsequent chapter on preaching, at Church of the Resurrection we don't use the lectionary assignments for scripture reading, but rather we develop themes that flow into sermon series, while keeping our worship rooted in the scripture text from which the sermon is being preached each week.

Tradition

In many of today's growing churches tradition has been discarded altogether. There is no mention of the liturgical year, or the great seasons of Lent and Advent. There are no religious symbols in worship, as these churches have believed such symbols might turn away nonreligious people. In one of the largest churches in America there is not even a cross present in the sanctuary. One large megachurch designed its sanctuary to look like a sports arena from the outside, feeling it would help attract the unchurched. This approach to "doing church" is unnecessary.

Our experience is that nonreligious and nominally religious people are not turned off by tradition, provided it is appropriately interpreted for them.

Our experience is that nonreligious and nominally religious people (who make up about 70 percent of those who join our church) are not turned off by tradition, provided it is appropriately interpreted for them. They are not afraid of sacred architecture, provided it is intentionally designed to welcome, express joy, and enhance community. In fact, when the significance of the altar, the candles, the liturgical year, baptism, and the Eucharist is explained, there is a deep appreciation of these elements of worship and a wonderful sense of connecting with Christians through the centuries. In addition, many of the hymns of the church have a richness and spiritual and theological depth that is not found in contemporary praise songs.

The key for unlocking the treasures of some of the more traditional elements of worship—the symbols, the sacraments, and the traditional hymns—is to interpret, explain, and ade-

quately set them up. We teach our children about the significance of the various acts of worship both in Sunday school and
in confirmation. I preach sermons from time to time explaining
the various elements of worship. We explain the significance of
hymns, and talk about the meaning of baptism each week.
Several years ago our choir performed Mendelssohn's *Elijah*.
Knowing that this is not the style of music most of our members
listen to, and that the words are a bit hard to understand if you
don't know the story, we preached a four-week series of sermons on Elijah, utilizing the sets used in the oratorio. We
introduced some of the music from *Elijah* in worship during
those weeks, in the anthem slot. By the time the choir performed
the oratorio our members knew the story and were able to savor
this musical masterpiece. Had the choir simply spent months
working on this piece, and performed it without this preparation, it would still have been a nice performance, but it would
have missed the ministry opportunity in which people's faith
was transformed.

We do very little liturgical reading in worship. We find that
for many people it is difficult to fully engage their hearts in these
acts of worship, and too easy to simply read the responses
without truly entering into worship.

Tradition, sacred symbols, hymns, and sacraments can and
should have an important place in our worship, and can be quite
powerful. The key is translating and interpreting these elements
for our people.

Experience

For most of us, reality and truth is experienced, not simply
understood. When it comes to worship this means that we want
to *feel* something when we worship. It is for this reason that the
charismatic and Pentecostal churches saw such explosive
growth in the last century.

As a young person I came to faith in Christ is such a church.
Though it has been nearly twenty years since I was last a part of
a church like this, I can still say that many of the profound
experiences of the presence of God that I have had in worship
were in these churches. This is primarily a result of the music

that is used in worship—music that begins with high-energy songs of praise, and then moves to quiet and more reflective songs, sung to God, rather than about God, often taken directly from the individual psalms of praise. We in the mainline have often been skeptical of such music, fearful that worship leaders were merely manipulating people emotionally rather than allowing the Holy Spirit to genuinely work. It is true that this often happens in such settings. At the same time we have forgotten how much we appreciate such experiences in other settings.

Not long ago I attended a concert featuring Elton John and Billy Joel. The arena was filled with eighteen thousand baby boomers and it was, for many, a near religious experience. I watched in amazement as nearly everyone joined in on their favorite songs, singing aloud, clapping to the music, and obviously enjoying every moment. As the show neared the end, and the final encores were being played, the back-up bands left the stage and John and Joel then shared two of their more reflective songs, "Candle in the Wind" and "Piano Man." Eighteen thousand people put their arms around one another and swayed to Joel's "Piano Man" leaving the concertgoers on a high that they would carry with them for several days.

But what will these same people find when they attend our mainline churches for worship? What will they experience there? Will it move them? Will they *feel* anything? The danger, of course, in even asking these questions is that we can focus so much on feelings and experiences that worship loses all integrity and theological grounding. But in some ways we have always asked these questions. The great symbols and forms of worship and sacred architecture of the past all were designed to help worshipers experience God. From the soaring gothic arches of the European cathedrals, to the incense, chants, and icons of the Orthodox churches of the East, to the fast moving hymns of the Wesleys coupled with its "low church" liturgy, worship and the worship setting were designed to help people experience God. The challenge today is that the generation most mainline churches have lost is a generation that experiences God in ways that are not synonymous with the ways people born before World War II often experience God.

At Church of the Resurrection most worshipers feel several things throughout the course of the services (regardless of whether the services are our traditional or contemporary services). They will feel excitement and anticipation as they enter; most people come expecting to meet God and to receive something that will help them grow in their faith. The energy level is then raised by our introduction to worship and the time of greeting when we welcome one another. From here we try to quiet things down for a moment, to reflect on why we've come together. Then worship begins with a high-energy praise song, hymn, or choral piece. We sing three hymns in a row, trying to allow time for worshipers to begin to praise. We also allow time for silent prayer before the pastoral prayer is offered. At least once a month we sing the Lord's Prayer in a call and response. The anthems are chosen, in part, based upon both traditional and contemporary music that will speak to our congregation. The sermon is delivered with passion and conviction. The offertory is meant to serve as a continuation of the sermon's theme. And the final benediction is aimed to send the worshipers forth on a high note with a bit of passion and enthusiasm.

> Our aim is to allow worship to be more than just cognitive and traditional by also letting it be experiential and contemporary.

Does worship always follow this pattern? No. Does our worship always succeed in facilitating people's experience of God's presence? No. But our aim is to allow worship to be more than just cognitive and traditional by also letting it be experiential and contemporary.

Reason

While many enjoyed the feeling and emotion of the charismatic and Pentecostal expressions of worship, substance and depth and intellectually satisfying music and preaching were sometimes lacking in these churches. Many of the mainline churches staked this out as their domain. Unfortunately even the mainline churches often offered little more than "fluff," the difference being that our fluff was boring and low energy!

It is common to speak of today's young people—those under thirty—as "postmoderns." Part of the defining characteristics of postmodernity is thought to be a deemphasis on reason and intellect in favor of experience. To the degree that many long to experience reality, I would agree. But if this is meant to say that postmoderns are not interested in topics such as apologetics and theology, and that they don't enjoy hearing a well-reasoned presentation of the gospel, I would strongly disagree. My experience with those under thirty indicates that they are looking for and value both experience *and* reason. They want both a gospel that makes sense and one that is emotionally and spiritually satisfying.

Both the nonreligious and the deeply committed Christians enjoy learning and being intellectually stimulated in worship. A common characteristic among rapidly growing churches is the feeling that participants actually learn something while in worship. One church I recently visited had ports underneath the first few rows of pews for laptop computer users to plug into so they could take notes and download the pastor's sermon and resources while they were listening in worship.

Worship Planning

At Church of the Resurrection we have a team of people who help plan worship. This includes our lead music staff, our pastors, our video team leader, our worship coordinator, my assistant, and myself. We meet for two hours each Monday. We begin by reviewing what happened in the prior week's worship services, noting any improvements or changes that need to be made. Then we look ahead eight weeks, spending a few minutes on each week. We do this because the music and video teams do best with at least two months' lead time to work on their projects for worship. Once we've planned this part of worship eight weeks in the future, we back up until we get to the upcoming weekend in worship. During this meeting I outline the ideas I have for the sermon and invite sharing about other ideas, illustrations, or concepts that might be brought into the sermon. From this information, the music department is able to choose hymns and praise songs, the pastors are able to write their pastoral prayers, and I am ready to write my sermon. I will describe this process more fully in chapter 9.

Prayer

One last element of worship that must not be ignored is prayer. Each week the worship team begins its work praying for God's direction and leadership in our meeting and in worship. Throughout the week the team prays for the worship services that weekend. Before worship begins I am usually kneeling in prayer in the sanctuary inviting the Holy Spirit to work in and through everyone who is playing a role in worship. I pray for the ushers, greeters, sound and lighting technicians, camera operators, nursery workers, musicians, pastors, and all others who are making worship happen. I pray for the people who will be coming to worship. And I pray that God will help me to worship, rather than simply lead worship. I ask that God will take over and, in the midst of my preaching or worship leading, make me invisible so that people don't see or hear me, but instead hear from God. I am convinced that prayer is a critical part of offering Spirit-empowered worship that transforms people's lives.

As you consider your worship services, how would unchurched persons in their twenties, thirties, or forties describe your services? What are the weakest points in your worship services? What are the strengths? When was the last time you explained the significance of the various symbols you use in worship? Of the sacraments? How would average worshipers in your congregation describe their experiences as they leave the service each week?

In the next chapter let's take a look at the sermon itself.

NINE

Preaching

Preaching is at one and the same time the activity pastors love, and dread. There is nothing like standing before a congregation knowing that you have something worth saying—a word from God for their lives, a word that is relevant, about which you are passionate, and for which you are prepared to speak. To preach with conviction and passion and to watch the facial expressions of the congregation, to see that they are listening intently, that they are hearing the word, and that God is speaking to them; it simply does not get any better than this. Such preaching is exhilarating. Part of the joy of this experience is that you are being used by God; God is at work in that moment of preaching and you are the mouthpiece. Even as I write these words I can feel the excitement of the preaching experience.

Yet preaching is also dreadful! Each week the pastor must hear from God, must study and prepare so that when Sunday comes the word that is delivered is relevant, fresh, inspiring, well-prepared, and faithful to the scripture from which it is drawn. There will be an entire congregation gathered to listen—a congregation expecting God to speak through you. And every pastor knows the feeling of showing up on Sunday not having adequately prepared, not feeling you have an authentic and relevant word to share, and sensing, as you are preaching, that you are not connecting. I have at times wanted to apologize after the sermon saying, "Please come back next week. I know that today's message was not as helpful as it could have been." And though we comfort ourselves as pastors with stories of parishioners who come up after those particularly poor sermons to tell us that it was "your best sermon ever," we also know that many of those folks are just being compassionate. It is a horrible thing to stand in the pulpit to preach and have nothing worth saying. And most pastors have been there.

This leads me to ask the questions, "What is preaching, *really*?" and, "What is the intention of a sermon?" When we look to the New Testament we go first to the model that Jesus offers us. Only a fraction of Jesus' first sermons is preserved for us in the Gospels. We read in Mark 1:14-15, "After John was put in prison, Jesus went into Galilee, proclaiming the good news of God. 'The time has come,' he said. 'The kingdom of God is near. Repent and believe the good news!'" From this and other sermon fragments of Jesus preserved in the Gospels we find the following characteristics:

1. Urgency ("The time has come")
2. Conviction (all of Jesus' messages are preached with absolute conviction)
3. Proclamation of theological and spiritual truth ("the kingdom of God is near")
4. A clear invitation to respond to the message ("Repent and believe the good news!")
5. A basic orientation and conviction that theological truth is always good news (mentioned twice in these two verses)
6. Utilized stories from the life experience of the hearers (especially so in the parables)
7. Was surprisingly "seeker sensitive"; that is, Jesus offered grace and compassion to the lost in his message ("Come to me, all you who are weary and burdened" in Matthew 11:28 (NIV) and "The Son of Man came to seek out and to save the lost" in Luke 19:10)
8. Was prophetic and confrontational toward those who considered themselves religious, challenging such believers to move beyond the letter of the Law to the heart and spirit of the Law
9. Was practical, dealing with real-life issues that people struggled with (worry, materialism, marriage and divorce, hatred, forgiveness, and ill will)
10. Taught persons how to connect with God (dealing with issues of prayer, fasting, worship, giving, and other matters of how one practices one's faith).

We must make these same characteristics a part of our preaching today.

There are a host of wonderful books written on preaching. My own preaching style has no doubt been influenced by these, as well as by watching and listening to various preachers, and by reading sermons from great pulpiteers. At this point I cannot pinpoint the direct influences on the form my preaching takes. I know it has evolved a great deal since seminary and I have no doubt that it is still changing. I do feel I am a more effective preacher today than ever before. Since "preaching" is often listed among the top reasons nonreligious and nominally religious people join Church of the Resurrection, it seems appropriate to devote a chapter of this book to the subject. My aim is to include an overview of my philosophy of preaching, a description of the process I use to prepare sermons, and then a list of sermon ideas that might spark the reader's own creative process.

> Ask the average nonreligious person to tell you about preaching and sermons and you are likely to be disappointed. "Preaching" has a negative connotation for most of them.

I view the aim of my preaching to be an extension of the aim or purpose of our church. By way of reminder, Church of the Resurrection's purpose is to "build a Christian community where nonreligious and nominally religious people are becoming deeply committed Christians." The aim of my preaching mirrors this.

Ask the average nonreligious person to tell you about preaching and sermons and you are likely to be disappointed. "Preaching" has a negative connotation for most of them. It is something that self-righteous, narrow-minded people do *to* others. Sermons are equivalent to lectures, in the most negative sense of that word. When nonreligious persons do think of sermons in the context of a church service they often describe them as "long," "boring," or "irrelevant." I have often heard people describe a preacher as preaching "over my head." By this the layperson means that he did not understand the message the preacher was trying to give. I often hear these same people note apologetically that sermons are wonderful times to nod off!

I am sympathetic to these folks. I find it terribly hard to stay awake for most sermons I hear. What would it take to keep me awake and hold my attention? More important for most pastors are these questions: What would it take to keep our parishioners awake and hold their attention? And for those who are serious about reaching the unchurched, What would it take to keep the unchurched visitors awake and hold their attention?

Obviously the goal of effective preaching is not merely to keep people awake and to hold their attention. If this were the case we could easily find ways to accomplish this. We could offer stand-up comedy or tell fascinating story after fascinating story or use clip after clip from Hollywood films, all of which might hold the congregation's attention, but none of which, in and of itself, would necessarily make for great *preaching*.

In listening to laypeople speak about what characteristics make a sermon more or less effective I often hear the following: Effective sermons are interesting, relevant, biblical, under-standable, offer clear application to the hearer's daily life, address real-life issues, and are preached with conviction, passion, love, integrity, and humility. When this combination of characteristics comes together, the preacher will connect the truth of the Scriptures with congregation members' lives in a way that will transform the entire church.

The Five Aims of Preaching

My aim is to accomplish the following in preaching: evangelism, discipleship, equipping and sending, pastoral care, and institutional development. I develop preaching plans for two years at a time (more about this below). As I look over the sermon series I have planned, my aim is to be sure that I have covered all of these aims somewhere during the year. My hope is to accomplish most of these goals in each sermon series I preach, though some will be more heavily weighted toward one or another of them. Ultimately my aim in preaching is to help the congregation to become deeply committed Christians. I will now briefly examine each of the above aims of preaching in more detail.

Evangelism

The two times when unchurched people are most likely to attend worship are Easter and Christmas. This comes as no surprise. Unfortunately many pastors turn the Christmas Eve and Easter weekends over to the music department for cantatas, leaving the sermon out altogether. One pastor I knew invited guest preachers along with his own associate pastors to preach on Christmas Eve! While music can be a powerful evangelistic tool, seldom will the finest cantata speak to an unchurched person the way a well-crafted evangelistic sermon will speak to them. At Easter and Christmas our music department provides outstanding music *and* I preach the very best sermons I can preach.

Our members know that Easter and Christmas are for the unchurched and that the sermons will be very basic. They will be aimed at helping nonreligious or nominally religious persons to understand the significance of Easter or Christmas for their daily lives. They will typically include one or two moving stories about what the gospel looks like in the daily lives of real people in our church (from whom I procure permission to tell their stories). I aim to be gentle but persuasive. My hope is to teach and inspire the unchurched to want to know more about Christ. My hope is to be used by the Holy Spirit to create in the unchurched a deep hunger to want to know more. These sermons include a touch of apologetics coupled with a heavily existential component.

At Christmas Eve candlelight services each year we, the staff at Church of the Resurrection, announce, through a full-color postcard inserted in each bulletin and a short video promotion shown at the beginning of each service, what the January–February series of sermons will be. We call our January–February sermon series our "fishing expedition sermons." Our aim is to offer something that will be so interesting, and will so clearly speak to the issues the unchurched have, that they will want to join us for services beginning the second weekend in January. (The first weekend in January is usually a poorly attended weekend since many of our people are out of town while their kids are on break, so we postpone the launch of the sermon series until the next weekend.) Two examples of sermon series will suffice: On Christmas Eve 1999 we announced that the January series would be "Christianity and the Controversial Issues of Our Time" (published as *Confronting the Controversies* by Abingdon Press in 2001). Sermon topics included the death penalty, euthanasia, abortion, and homosexuality, among others. When we began the sermons in January worship attendance increased by more than one thousand per weekend over attendance in November, as those who attended Christmas Eve returned for this series. Likewise, at Christmas Eve 2000 we announced the January 2001 series, "Where Was God When . . . ?" focused on understanding how we can make sense of God in light of the tragic experiences of life. Once again worship attendance soared by another one thousand per weekend over the previous year's attendance. This series on tragedy addressed the number one question that keeps unchurched people from faith: Where is God when tragedy strikes?

What is interesting about these fishing expeditions is that our own members become very excited about them as well. First, they know that these are sermons designed to help them invite their friends to church. The sermons are easy to market to their friends because of the accessible themes. Our members will take extra copies of the postcards (we always have plenty of extra cards available for this purpose) and give them to their friends and coworkers. A beautician in our church displays the card in front of her mirror where she cuts hair so that all who come in can see it. But our members are not only excited because these topics are of interest to the unchurched. Rather, long-time Christians also wrestle with these same questions and they are grateful for a series of sermons addressing them.

Not all of our evangelistic preaching comes in the form of a fishing expedition series of sermons. In each series of sermons there will be individual messages that lend themselves to a conclusion in which we invite persons listening to make a decision to follow Christ. We do not currently invite persons to come forward in an "altar call." We believe many unchurched persons find this somewhat contrived. Instead, our invitation comes as we pray at the end of the sermon. We would say something like this, "As your heads are bowed, perhaps you know today that you want to follow Christ, to be one of his disciples. If so, the process for becoming a Christian begins with one simple step; it begins with your saying a prayer. Pray this prayer after me quietly, 'Jesus, I would like to be one of your disciples. I want to follow you. I invite you into my life. Please forgive me of my sins. Today, I have decided to entrust my life to you.

> **My experience in most mainline churches is that we talk about how wonderful it is to be a Christian, but we never help persons to actually "complete the loop" and give their lives to Christ.**

Thank you for accepting me and counting me as one of your people. Amen.'" This simple prayer gives those ready to respond a way of expressing their desire, and a way of knowing that they have begun on this path. I break the prayer into short phrases so they can actually pray it after me. Many of our people have begun their walk with Christ with this prayer. In the future, when we have a prayer chapel constructed adjacent to the sanctuary, we will invite those who have prayed this prayer, who would like to talk with a pastor, to go there immediately following the service.

We have not always given such an invitation. But my experience in most mainline churches is that, in marketing terms, we never "ask for the sale." We talk about how wonderful it is to be a Christian, but we never help persons to actually "complete the loop" and give their lives to Christ. We assume this happens at membership, but many of those who have joined our churches have not personally invited Christ into their lives, even if they profess to be Christians with their membership vows.

We believe it is important to give people the opportunity and the means to express to God their desire to be Christians.

Hence, every four to six weeks we will extend this invitation at the end of a sermon.

One last note about evangelistic preaching: A perfect opportunity to give an invitation for people to accept Christ is on Holy Communion weekends. Some mainline churches offer the Eucharist every weekend; others, like many in The United Methodist Church, typically offer communion monthly. For all, this Sunday is a perfect opportunity to give an invitation.

One of the criticisms fundamentalists make of mainline churches is that we don't give "altar calls" as they give them. When one of these folks mentions this to me I am quick to tell them that mainline churches do give altar calls every time we have Holy Communion. For in the act of Holy Communion we ask persons to come forward (in our tradition, members come forward to receive the elements), and to visibly, tangibly, invite Christ into their lives, and to symbolize their acceptance of his death on the cross for their sins, his grace, and his presence in their lives, as they eat the bread and drink the wine. This is the invitation we give to our congregation every time we celebrate the Eucharist. After the Great Thanksgiving I say to our congregation, "This meal is your opportunity to express to God your desire to live for Christ, to receive Christ into your life, and to accept his mercy and grace. When you take the bread and the wine take this as an opportunity to rededicate your life to him." It is remarkable how this simple invitation has, for many, helped to transform Holy Communion from an empty ritual to a "means of grace."

Discipleship

Clearly the majority of sermons should be aimed at helping both the nonreligious and those who are quite religious to become deeply committed disciples. In order to accomplish this aim, the preacher must be clear about what a deeply committed disciple looks like and then he or she must determine what kind of sermons would help develop such disciples. As I mentioned in chapter 7, I have defined deeply committed disciples as those who love and serve God with their head, their heart, and who love God and their neighbor by serving others with their hands.

1. Loving God with the Mind

I have indicated that to love God with the head represents the cognitive aspect of the Christian life. It means growing in one's understanding of theology, the Scriptures, worship, the sacraments, the great traditions of the church and her history and its relationship to us today, and viewing the world in light of our faith. Throughout the Scriptures we are told to "grow in grace, *and in the knowledge* of our Lord"(2 Peter 3:18 KJV), or to "*study* to show thyself approved" (2 Timothy 2:15 KJV). While small groups represent good opportunities for church members and visitors to grow in the cognitive arena, there are two things mandating that this task must also be taken up by the preacher: First, in most mainline churches it is uncommon to find more than 50 percent of the adults who attend worship also attending adult Sunday school or some other small discipleship group. (Those churches where a high percentage of adults attend both worship and Sunday school tend to be older congregations.) Second, many of our small groups in mainline churches tend to place a higher value on fellowship than on study. Studies such as DISCIPLE and Christian Believer (both available from The United Methodist Publishing House) have certainly gone a long way in offering more intense learning opportunities, but the fact still remains that for many of the people in our pews, their primary source for Christian education will be the pulpit.

The preacher's task then is, in part, to help her or his flock to grow in the cognitive aspects of the faith. This dictates a strong teaching element to one's sermons. My aim in each message is to teach the congregation something that listeners may not have known, or which they may have forgotten. This includes teaching them how to do Christian ethics (as in the controversial issues series of sermons mentioned earlier), or our denominational distinctives, by not only teaching them the biblical material but also how to study the Scriptures. I have tried to teach them Christian theology, as in the series mentioned above on "Where Was God When . . . ?" in which our focus was on various conceptions of the doctrine of providence and in a recent series entitled "What Christians Believe and Why." I have found the use of video to be very helpful in this task when I am teaching things that otherwise might be a bit dull. When I am teaching material on the background of a biblical story, for instance, we will include slides projected through our video system of archaeological sites or maps or timelines. My hope is that our members will be stimulated by these sermons to dig deeper; that they will be able to "give an account of their faith" to others; that they will be informed Christians and that the information I offer them will help form them spiritually.

At the same time a sermon is not the same as a lecture. Every sermon I offer that is heavily weighted toward teaching will also have a strong element of preaching and invitation or challenge at the end. Recently I preached a sermon on the significance of baptism. We projected photos onto our video screens of baptisteries from the third century through the sixth century to help teach about the meaning of the sacrament. I surveyed the biblical literature and spent nearly twenty-five minutes teaching both the historical and biblical foundations of baptism. But the last eight minutes of the sermon moved from the didactic to the existential by discussing the significance of the various meanings of baptism for our daily lives. I ended by giving an invitation for those who had never been baptized to consider being baptized at our Easter vigil. In response we had 140 people who were baptized the night before Easter! These were children, youth, and adults who had never been baptized, for whom their baptisms now had an incredible significance as a result of the teaching of the sermon on baptism. There were persons who had converted from other faiths, persons who were leaving behind a lifetime of sin, and even persons who had been members of mainline churches all of their lives but had somehow never been baptized. (An additional use of this sermon has come as we now give an audiotape of it to all persons in our church prior to baptizing them.)

2. *Loving God with the Heart*

To love God with the heart is another way of talking about the interior life. In this case we aim to help our members experience a personal relationship with God that is transforming in nature. The preacher's task is both to inspire and motivate as well as to teach and equip the congregation to pursue the spiritual life. This includes teaching on the spiritual disciplines (as in a series of sermons we offered several years ago entitled, "The Ten Habits of Highly Effective Christians" or another on "Lessons on Prayer from the Life of Jesus"), as well as focusing on the existential aspects of the faith. Many of our sermons focus on knowing God intimately, on understanding and discerning God's will, on issues such as God's mercy, the work of the Holy Spirit, and what it means to live a life completely surrendered to Christ. In part the preacher will, by her or his preaching, paint a picture of God that helps parishioners see and perceive God and understand God's will for their lives, which is what Jesus aimed to do when he taught the people in parables.

Equipping and Sending Sermons: Loving God with the Hands

Part of the task of discipleship sermons takes us into another category of sermon altogether: the sermons aimed at equipping congregation members for service and inspiring them to listen for God's calling upon their lives. The task is to inspire, motivate, equip, and challenge parishioners to *do something* about their faith by serving their neighbors and serving the world. It is impossible to be a mature disciple without serving God and neighbor. In this vein our task is to teach about the gifts of the Holy Spirit and help persons discern which gifts God has equipped them with; to teach about the fruit of the Spirit; to teach about relationships and the role our faith plays in shaping them; to teach on issues like love, forgiveness, compassion, and service. To disciple your congregation in this way is to help congregation members see the connection between the biblical passages on justice and the way they live their lives personally and as members of society. This preaching helps congregation members hear God's call on their lives and motivates them, once this call is heard, to act upon it.

We have an entire sermon planned around inviting persons to listen for a call to full-time Christian service. We will be focusing on how one hears a call from God, how one discerns God's will, and the joys of full-time Christian service. We will give three ways for people to respond: First, for those who believe God may have a calling upon their lives, we will follow up by hosting an event with representatives of Saint Paul School of Theology (our local United Methodist seminary) and with members of the

> **One task of preaching is to inspire, motivate, equip, and challenge parishioners to *do something* about their faith by serving their neighbors and serving the world.**

Board of Ordained Ministry from our region (this is the board that works with candidates for ordination). Second, for those who do not believe they are called to be in full-time Christian service, we will focus on ways they can be in ministry in our local church and in mission agencies in volunteer capacities. Finally, we will invite persons to consider contributing to a scholarship fund for those who are interested in ordained ministry. We will include in this sermon video interviews with young seminary students and second-career pastors describing their calling and the joy they feel in ministry.

We believe that leadership continues to be a critical need in creating healthy and vital local churches and our hope is that through this sermon God will call gifted and talented people within our congregation to consider moving into local church leadership and ministry.

Pastoral Care

On any given Sunday I count on the fact that 25 percent of the people coming to worship need pastoral care. In a small congregation the pastor may be able to devote sufficient time in identifying and then working with these parishioners one-on-one. In a larger congregation this is impossible and many of the parishioners would not avail themselves of the opportunity even if it were available.

Here's a sampling of what the pastoral needs look like within my congregation each week: depression, marital infidelity, job loss, alcohol and drug addiction, grief from pregnancy loss, divorce and marriages on the verge of divorce, grief from the death of a loved one, persons facing cancer or other serious illness, infertility, rape and incest survivors, eating disorders, anxiety disorders, and a host of other pastoral care issues too numerous to mention. In your congregation there will be members wrestling with pastoral care issues this weekend. The question is, What will you do about it?

We preach on these issues on a regular basis asking the question, "What are the implications of our faith in Christ and what help might the Scriptures offer for those wrestling with these concerns?" Two years ago, after preaching the funeral of a young man who committed suicide, I devoted an entire sermon to suicide (a sermon that we have on tape at our tape table every week so that members can purchase a copy for themselves or friends who are contemplating suicide). A number of persons have said that this sermon alone helped them decide not to take their own lives. We offered a sermon on anxiety disorders and panic attacks after discovering that a significant number of men and women faced this debilitating struggle. Several years ago we offered a series of sermons called "Biblical Perspectives on Love, Sex, and Marriage." This series was prompted by a rash of pastoral visits with couples who were at the point of divorce. By the time I had seen them it was nearly too late. Frustrated, I wanted to help our congregation members understand a biblical perspective on marriage and the relationship between men and women. Interestingly enough, this series ended up being a "fishing expedition" as well because our members invited many of their nonchurched friends who were struggling with marital problems. Nearly two hundred new families began attending the church during this series.

These pastoral care sermons are important, and help us offer real hope and real help to those who are broken. Our tape ministry has been invaluable at this point. We now give a copy of the tapes on marriage to all couples who marry in our church. Often people will know someone who is wrestling with a particular topic, but who does not attend our church, or who lives out of town. I receive E-mail and letters from people across the country who have received copies of our sermons on tape, and who have written to say how helpful these sermons have been.

Institutional Development

Finally, there are sermons that a pastor must preach primarily to ensure the health and vitality of the church as an institution. These include sermons on the purpose of the church, sermons addressing the needs of the church, vision casting sermons, and stewardship sermons. (While stewardship sermons should be primarily about discipleship, most congregants will see them as institutional development sermons.) In September of each year I preach sermons that are focused on discipleship but which clearly lay out the expectations we have of our members (see chapter 7). One weekend a year our church has a mission focus weekend with a missions fair; the sermon, I hope, will help the congregation hear God's call to serve those outside the walls of the church.

While I make reference to our church's purpose statement at least once a month, three times each year I preach sermons that are focused on this statement and our mission as a church. On this point my experience mirrors that of Rick Warren (*The Purpose-Driven Church*): even the most committed Christians tend to lose sight of the missional purposes of the church. This is especially true in a setting where there are unpleasant side effects to growth. As a result of our rapid growth we have frequent problems with overcrowding in the parking lot and the nurseries, and difficulty moving through the hallways and narthex between services. Some of our ministries run at or over capacity and we have once again been forced to move some Sunday school classes off-site. All of these problems create a feeling that the church is getting "too big." It is important to note that preaching is an important tool in shaping the congregation's spirit and response to the overcrowded conditions. A well-timed sermon with a clear biblical focus and concrete illustrations of how the church has changed people's lives can take what would appear to be negative conditions and help the congregation see them as causes for rejoicing.

Another example of institutional development sermons includes those sermons that should be preached to prepare people for future challenges. These are usually combined with a sermon on the purpose of the church. Every time our congregation has prepared to move to a new worship site I have used the final Sunday in the existing worship location as an opportunity to let members know what they could expect. Each move came with both positive and negative consequences. One negative was that the new place of worship was always larger and less intimate than the existing place of worship. Of course that was why we were moving, to make room for more people. But you cannot underestimate the difficulty congregants experience in giving up intimacy and in experiencing change. One positive was that there would be more room and that meant that someone's father or mother or sister or brother who did not know Christ would now have a seat.

One final word about institutional development sermons. These should be preached sparingly. If congregants, especially the nonreligious and nominally religious, feel that the pastor is always preaching sermons about the church and its needs, they will soon recognize the congregation as one that is inwardly focused and primarily concerned about its own survival needs rather than the needs of people.

What About the Lectionary?

Many mainline pastors utilize the Revised Common Lectionary, a system of assigned scripture readings for each Sunday of the year operating on a three-year cycle. This is what I was taught in seminary and there are many advantages to using the lectionary as the basis for preaching. My first few years in the ministry were spent preaching using this method. I ultimately abandoned lectionary preaching for several reasons. First I found that the lectionary provided little opportunity for my flock to determine what it needed to hear. Instead my flock was bound to hear whatever was prescribed by the lectionary on a given weekend. While some pastors are adept at taking the lectionary readings and helping them say what the congregation needs to hear, this can abuse the scriptures. Second, I felt that the relationship between the various readings on a given weekend was often obtuse. Third, while some of the lectionary readings do offer continuity for a season, many of the readings are marked by discontinuity, especially if a pastor moves from the Gospel reading one week to the Old Testament or Psalm the next. Fourth, I found that people are drawn to preaching that starts with their human condition and needs and then applies the gospel to their situation in life, rather than preaching that starts with a pre-assigned scripture reading and then seeks to find a creative application. Finally, I found that people were drawn to a sermon series and to upcoming sermons that tie into that series (we advertise what the sermons will be for the upcoming month), especially if we have started with their needs or interests. I am aware that many reading this book are excellent lectionary preachers and that there are a host of wonderful resources for those who use the lectionary. I am also aware that most of the churches that attract large crowds of nonreligious people and introduce them to Christ do not use the lectionary.

The Sermon Writing Process

There is no one activity that a pastor does that can have a greater influence on the vitality of the congregation than preaching. If a pastor is a poor preacher and does not devote sufficient time to preparing sermons, the entire congregation will suffer. If a pastor prepares well-researched and thoughtful sermons, with clear relevance and application for her or his congregants, and delivers them with passion, conviction, and clarity, the entire congregation will reap the benefits. Furthermore, in no other activity are so many people affected at one time by the pastor's ministry as they are during the sermon in Sunday worship. *Since this is the case, there is nothing more important than providing sufficient time to prepare excellent sermons.*

Today my sermon planning looks something like this: Every July the church grants me two weeks of study-leave for prayer, reading, research, sermon planning, and outlining. In addition, twice each year I take a two-day retreat at a local camp to update my sermon plan and seek God's directions for the coming months. I ask myself several questions as I begin this process:

- What do members of my flock need to hear?
- Where do they need to grow?
- What are they struggling with?
- What is happening in our world that might affect or be affected by their faith?
- What do they fear?
- What part of the Scriptures or theological or spiritual focuses have I neglected?

In asking these questions, I begin clarifying the direction the upcoming sermons need to take. I spend hours praying (usually taking long walks as I pray). I read from the Scriptures. In the process of these prayer walks I find my creativity opened up. I come back to the lodge and begin brainstorming ideas for series' themes. From a list of these I settle in on eight or nine that I will then enter on my computer with a brief description of what I was visualizing for the series and the rationale behind it. I then try to develop six to eight individual sermon titles for each series. Finally, I outline each sermon, beginning with the human condition, moving to possible scriptures that might speak to this condition and any theological concepts that have bearing on it. I then begin to give thought to possible supporting material including illustrations and hymns.

When I come back from retreat I will provide each member of our worship planning team a copy of these outlines, which will have detailed information on the next two or three sermon series, and sketchier information on sermon series to be preached over the course of the next two years. I ask the worship team members to critique the ideas, share their thoughts, and see which series they are excited about and which they find dull or irrelevant. At this meeting we will finalize plans for the sermons during the coming year.

As I mentioned briefly in chapter 8, our worship team meets together on Monday mornings from 10:00 A.M. until noon. Because all of our teams seek to function as small groups as well, we begin with sharing joys and concerns and praying for one another. Our worship planning team includes the senior pastor, two associate pastors who oversee our caring ministries, our director of music ministries, our assistant director of music who works with our contemporary music ministries, our worship coordinator (she oversees ushers, greeters, communion, banners, and other logistical functions related to worship), our executive pastor responsible for music and worship ministries, our director of video ministries, and my executive assistant. We launch into our planning by evaluating our prior weekend's worship. Our aim is to continually improve what we do in worship. Each week there is something that didn't go as we had planned the prior weekend. Following this discussion we begin looking at worship six to eight weeks out, and then we back up each week until we come to the current week's worship services.

In these meetings I share what I have completed in the way of sermons for each of those weeks. From there our music people try to pull together anthems, offertories, special music, and hymns and praise songs that tie in with the themes. Our video team goes into action after these meetings brainstorming possible sermon starters or illustrations for video use. Our pastors use the information gained to help in writing their pastoral prayers. My assistant comes away from the meetings prepared to do some preliminary research on the Internet from which she will start files based upon the upcoming sermons. I come away from our worship planning meetings with insights and ideas that help in the final sermon writing.

Most pastors will not have the luxury of having a staff of this size to serve on a worship planning team. Even so a worship planning team may be formed of laypeople who have interests or passions in these various areas. There are laity in your church who would love to do research for you on the Internet. There are movie buffs who would love to brainstorm with others by E-mail to uncover possible movie scenes that might be used as illustrations in your messages. And there are music leaders and choir members who would be honored to help search for hymns tied into your messages.

After I leave the worship planning meeting my next stop is the sanctuary to pray. I usually try to walk through each section of chairs, asking God to guide me so that I might know what he would say to those who will be sitting in these seats in worship this weekend. I invite the Holy Spirit to guide me, direct me, and speak to me as I begin preparing the sermon. Following this time of prayer I head to my house to work on the sermon from my home study. I work at home because I have found I cannot concentrate in my office with phones ringing and conversations happening just outside my door.

I spend Monday afternoon and late evening reading, usually from five to seven hours. I begin with the human condition we are exploring, clarifying what it is and searching for examples of this. I may read a host of articles from journals taken from the public library system's Internet site. Once I have sufficiently clarified the issues, I move to searching the Scriptures for the solution. This may be done with the help of books from my library on these themes. (Often before I launch into a series I will purchase key books relating the issues to the scriptures using a fund the church provides for books and continuing education.) These books may be the starting point for my own search of the Scriptures. As I begin to understand possible approaches to the topic from the Scriptures, I outline these on legal notepads. During this time I once more approach God in prayer, seeking discernment and opening myself to God's will and voice.

Once I have begun to understand how the Bible approaches the issue or topic, I will dig deeper by opening the commentaries to see if they can shed some light on my research to date. By Monday night this is generally where I am.

On Tuesdays I will have another three to four hours to work on my sermon. Here I begin to write a first draft, and sometimes even a second, of the sermon. By day's end I have a pretty strong leaning on where I am going with it, but the sermon is still far from complete. Late Wednesday night I will make another stab at completing a manuscript. On Thursday night I will do this again, and will finalize the sermon outline for the printed sermon notes as well as write a daily scripture reading and study guide to go along with the sermon, both of which will appear in the bulletin that weekend. On Saturdays I often will spend two to three more hours rewriting the final draft of my sermon, after which I will practice preaching it once through. My aim, once the sermon is written, is to be able to preach without referring to my manuscript. This is generally not that difficult if the sermon has a structure that makes sense.

Sermon Notes and Study Guides

As briefly referenced above, we include a one-page outline of the sermon complete with the scripture text, and, on the reverse side of the outline, a one-page study guide with daily scripture readings assigned along with a brief commentary and application of the scriptures that will be read.

Many churches use sermon outlines. I have found these are helpful in getting people to focus and remember the sermon. Our outlines usually include some "fill in the blank" spots, and we always include the answers to these blanks at the bottom of the page for those who don't take notes, or who miss the answer. In school I had a diffi-cult time remembering lectures if I did not take notes. I believe the same is true of ser-mons.

> My goal in prescribing a daily scripture reading and then offering some commentary on it was aimed at helping nominally religious people to experience success in reading the Bible.

While the sermon notes are common, the study guide we offer is innovative. When we began doing this I was not aware of another church utilizing this approach. It sprang from two different motives. First, because we have so many new Christians in the church, biblical illiteracy is very high. I wanted to change that. I wanted our members to actually read their Bibles daily and to use this discipline to grow in their faith. But when nominally churched people try to read the Bible they are often frustrated, believing that they cannot understand it. My goal in prescribing a daily scripture reading and then offering some commentary on it was aimed at helping these nominally religious people to experience success in reading the Bible. By assigning scriptures that are relatively easy to understand, and then by providing explanatory notes and questions aimed at helping them apply the scripture to their daily lives, I hope to help those who use the study guide to come to love reading the Scriptures.

Second, when I am finished researching my sermon there is always so much more I wish I could say. I could easily preach an hour each week, though our congregation would have a tough time sitting still for it! So, the study guide gives me an opportunity to include the information I would have liked to have included in my sermon if there had been more time. Thus the study guide follows the sermon, taking people deeper into the themes of the message.

We post the study guide on the church's website every Monday at *www.cor.org* so that our members who travel can still download the lessons and study the scriptures. We recently surveyed the congregation to see if members were actually using the guides. We discovered that 54 percent of our attenders were using them! Prior to the implementation of these guides I would have been surprised if more than 20 percent of our attenders spent time in daily scripture reading. It has been a huge success. One additional note: We ask our staff to use the study guides if they are not pursuing some other form of daily scripture study.

Sermon Ideas from Church of the Resurrection

Perhaps it might be helpful to actually examine a year of sermons to see how all of this fits together. In August 1999 I went on a three-day retreat and outlined sermons for the year 2000. At that time the church had experienced significant growth, moving from two thousand in attendance per weekend in 1997 to four thousand in attendance per weekend in 1999. Nearly 70 percent of these persons were nonreligious or nominally religious before coming to our church. As I considered the needs of our congregation it seemed that one of the most important things I could do was to lay a foundation for these newcomers. You can see how we aimed to do this as you look over the series for the year.

January–February 2000: Christianity and the Controversial Issues of Our Time

This series was our fishing expedition for 2000. It was announced on Christmas Eve 1999 and postcards were sent to all on our mailing list. Worship attendance increased by 20 percent and a new record was set on the final Sunday when worship passed six thousand for a nonholiday weekend. My aim was not simply to appeal to the nonreligious, but to teach our own congregation how to do Christian ethics while I also sought to offer them pastoral care. Each of these emphases can be seen in the individual topics covered:

The Separation of Church and State
Teaching Evolution in the Public Schools
Dr. Kevorkian and Euthanasia
Prayer in Public Schools
The Death Penalty
Gambling
Abortion
Homosexuality

March–April 2000: Portraits of Jesus from the Gospel of Luke

Every year, our Lenten sermon series is aimed specifically at taking our existing members deeper in their faith. In 2000 our aim was to help those who were new Christians to know the basic outline of Jesus' life and to learn of his heart and character while studying the Gospel of Luke. We challenged all of our worshipers to read through the entire Gospel of Luke during Lent and provided them with daily study guides and readings to help them accomplish this. The sermon titles included:

The Early Years
Wrestling with the Devil
The People Jesus Loved
The Women in His Life
The Gathering Storm
The Crucifixion
From Tragedy to Triumph: Easter

May–June 2000: Insights for Living from the Life of David

This series of sermons was actually prompted by pastoral care concerns within the congregation. As I began to look at the pastoral needs of our members I was reminded of the story of King David, who experienced both great triumphs and terrible tragedies. I had never preached an entire series of sermons on David before and I saw this as an opportunity to both address the pastoral care needs while teaching our congregation about this man who towers over the Old Testament, eclipsed only by Moses in importance to Israel's faith. I thoroughly enjoyed this series and found it stimulating to research, prepare, and preach. Topics included:

God's Unlikely Heroes (Samuel anoints David the
  shepherd boy)
Doing Battle with Giants (David defeats Goliath)
Ruth: Woman of Courage and Character (for Mother's
  Day)
Stabbed in the Back (Saul tries to destroy David and
  David's response)
The Qualities of True Friendship (David and Jonathan)
What a Tangled Web (David and Bathsheba)
For the Love of God: David and His Psalms
Problem Children and Struggling Parents (David as a
  father [Father's Day])
David's Last Words and Legacy

July 2000: The Power of the Holy Spirit

As I was planning this year's sermons I was aware that it had been some time since we focused specifically on the work of the Holy Spirit, despite the fact that the Holy Spirit is essential to experiencing the fullness of the Christian life. Knowing that our most committed members are those who are present during July when many of our less committed members take off for the lake, we decided to offer this series at that time. The series had a heavier teaching component than most of our series and this seemed a time when we could do this kind of teaching without losing the newer Christians. Sermons included:

The Holy Spirit in the Old and New Testaments

The Baptism of the Holy Spirit and the Ecstatic Gifts of the Spirit

DISCIPLE Bible Study Sunday (Every July we set aside one Sunday to have laypeople share their testimonies about DISCIPLE Bible Study as a way of inspiring and motivating our members to sign up for the fall session of DISCIPLE DISCIPLE is a thirty-two-week intensive Bible study. This Sunday might be considered a "Laity Sunday" since the laity share the message that day. This represents an institutional development sermon that is also focused on discipleship. The results are tremendous. Our growth in registration for DISCIPLE has outpaced our church's growth every year.)

The Equipping Gifts of the Holy Spirit

The Fruit of the Spirit

Walking with the Holy Spirit in our Daily Lives

August–October 2000: Sermons on the Narrow Path: The Teachings of Jesus for Today's World

This series of sermons would complete our goal of introducing our newer members to Jesus Christ. The prior series focused on the life of Jesus. This series focused on his words and message. Again we invited members to use their daily study guides in order to read nearly all of the teachings of Jesus found in the Gospels. Part of this series, held in September, coincided with our annual emphasis on our membership expectations, during which we encourage and challenge our members to get involved in a small group, find an area of service within the congregation, and become involved in mission ministries. Notice, too, how we took Jesus' teachings and focused them on the life situations that many of our people face. In this series of sermons we covered nearly every type of sermon listed above. I've included in parentheses a word or two about what type of sermon each of these was meant to be.

> Introduction to Jesus' Teaching: The Kingdom of God (This was a discipleship and teaching sermon, helping worshipers understand the concept of the kingdom of God in all of its dimensions.)
>
> Seventy Times Seven: Forgiving Others and Loving Your Enemies (This was a pastoral care sermon aimed at helping worshipers understand and live forgiveness.)
>
> The Golden Rule: Do Unto Others . . . (This was a basic discipleship sermon with a touch of pastoral care and Christian ethics.)
>
> Higher Up and Farther In: The Narrow Road (This was a discipleship sermon, but its focus was on moving people to become involved in a small group and it corresponded with a weekend emphasis on adult Sunday school, hence this was also an institutional development sermon.)
>
> The First Shall Be Last: Humility and Servanthood (This was an equipping/sending sermon but also an institutional development sermon. The weekend this was preached was the weekend we had invited our members to sign up for their areas of service for the coming year.)
>
> To the Least of These: The Sheep and the Goats (This was another equipping/sending sermon but also

an institutional development sermon. This was
our annual missions fair weekend in which mission agencies from throughout the metropolitan
Kansas City area set up booths in our narthex recruiting persons to serve in their ministries.)
Don't Worry, Be Happy: Worry and Anxiety (This was
a pastoral care sermon focused in part on issues
related to panic attacks and anxiety disorders.)
You Are the Light of the World (This was our tenth an-
niversary weekend for our church and an opportunity to recast the vision and remind the
congregation of our purpose, thus it was an institutional development sermon.)
Take the Log Out: Do Not Judge Others (This was
both a pastoral care and discipleship sermon.)
Prodigal Children: God's Mercy and Love (This was
an evangelism sermon with a clear invitation for
persons who had lived their lives as prodigals to
come back to God and to restore their relationship
with him.)
The Most Important Commandments: Love the
Lord . . . Love Your Neighbor (As the series finale
this was both an overview of all of Jesus' teachings as well as an evangelistic sermon.)

November 2000: Managing ~~YOUR~~ HIS Money: Sermons on Biblical Stewardship

My hope in this series was to look beyond the annual pledge
campaign and to help our members and visitors grow in their
understanding of biblical stewardship. Titles included:

The Rich Young Man
For Mature Audiences Only (the biblical tithe)
The Power of a Grateful Heart

For Advent 2000 the idea I had originally conceived for this
series did not materialize, so I went back to the lectionary and
used the Advent readings to help our congregation understand
the significance of Advent and Christmas.

One last word about preaching must be said. There is an element of effective preaching that goes beyond preparation and planning and even skillful writing. It is what our Pentecostal brothers and sisters call "the anointing." The anointing is the presence of the Holy Spirit in our preaching that takes our efforts to a whole new level, a level we could not arrive at on our own. The preacher and the congregation can sense it. It is experienced as power and an almost palpable sense that God is speaking. It is what I pray for each week, "Holy Spirit, please take over. Fill me, use me, and speak through me. Help me become invisible so that these people will see you instead."

We cannot control the Holy Spirit, but we can suppress the Spirit's work in our preaching. On a recent Christmas Eve we held eight candlelight services. I had worked very hard on my sermon all week. I had written a passable sermon, one I hoped would be effective in unpacking the significance of the Incarnation for the thousands of people who would be present for worship. But as I walked up to the church to get ready for the first service I felt God speaking to me in that "still small voice" that I have come to recognize. God said, "You didn't spend the amount of time in prayer that this service warrants." Tinged with guilt I said aloud, "You are right, Lord. I am so sorry. I was preparing this sermon as though this congregation were coming to hear from me, not as though they were coming to hear from you."

I went in the sanctuary and tried to make up for lost time. I got on my knees and prayed. I walked through the building and prayed. But by this time these were the desperate measures of a preacher who was trying to coax God into making up for my deficiencies. I preached the first four services, and the sermon was passable, the crowds seemed appreciative. My wife attended one of these services and indicated that the sermon was good. But I knew that "the anointing" was not there. But then came the fifth service, the service when most of the visitors attend, and I could tell there was something different. Despite having an overflow crowd, there came a moment in the sermon where God just took over. People were quiet and listening, eagerly awaiting what would come next. My preaching had a power to it that it had not had before. There were many in tears in the sanctuary. From that time forward throughout the evening there was something special that was happening in these services. Afterward my wife said, "That wasn't even the same sermon you preached earlier." In fact, it was the same exact material but it was transformed and empowered by the Holy Spirit. That night, after the last of eight services, I felt God was saying, "I anointed you tonight, despite the fact that you were unprepared, because these are my people. But I wanted you to sense the difference between your preaching and mine."

I am not sure what you will do with this. But I know the experience is real. It is a pure joy to preach when the Holy Spirit is a part of the preaching moment. At the same time I have come to dread those times when I don't sense the anointing. And the difference between these two is the amount of quality time spent during the week in prayer.

TEN

Pastoral Care

Although preaching may be the most important thing a pastor does to minister to his or her flock, pastoral care is where the lives of individual parishioners are most dramatically touched with the healing and transforming power of Christ. The church is the body of Christ, the physical incarnation of Jesus in the world today. Jesus spent a great deal of his time healing those with physical, spiritual, and emotional wounds and illnesses. He had compassion on those who were hurting, and sought to make them whole. If this was an important part of Jesus' ministry, it must be an important part of our ministry.

I have considered it the greatest privilege of my ministry to be with parishioners during their times of personal crisis or need. But I must admit that, at times, I have also found this ministry to be daunting. When I first graduated from seminary and began my ministry as a young associate pastor I would walk down the hospital corridors feeling completely inept. My seminary professors never told me what to say when I sat down with a parishioner who was dying of cancer, or who had just discovered he had AIDS. I searched through my library of seminary texts for the book that would give me the right words to offer when I arrived at the home of parents whose child had just committed suicide, or when I was called in the middle of the night to visit with a member whose husband had just left her for another woman. I admit that today, thousands of pastoral calls later, I often still feel completely inadequate for the task. The truth is, I don't have the "magic words" to alleviate another's suffering. My prayers are not guaranteed to bring healing and deliverance. I do not have the spiritual recipe to repair marriages or help children behave. What I have to offer is God's love and compassion, a hand to hold, ears to listen, a prayer shared in faith, scriptural principles and promises that can be a "lamp to one's feet and a light to one's path," and hope.

One of the most important lessons I try to remember in giving pastoral care comes from James 1:19: "You must understand this, my beloved: let everyone be quick to listen [and] slow to speak." While this verse was initially related to exercising caution in becoming angry, I find it is also wonderful advice for pastoral care. Part of the role of being an effective shepherd is simply being a good listener.

One evening I was visiting the convalescent center where one of my elderly parishioners lived. I knew that her life was drawing near an end. As we began to talk she asked if I would like to see her family photo albums. For the next forty-five minutes she told me her life story through pictures and she reminisced about the many things she was grateful for in her life. I just listened; that was my ministry to her. At the end of this time we prayed together, thanking God for all of the blessings represented by these photographs, and then we committed our lives to Christ for his keeping. As I prepared to leave I gently hugged Ruth, told her what a privilege it was to be her pastor, and said good-bye. As I left she lay down to rest. She died that night in her sleep. Ruth had no other family left. That evening my ministry was to listen and to reminisce with her, to help her thank God for the blessings, and to commit her life to his care.

When I offer pastoral care, my aim is always to *represent* Christ. I pray before entering a hospital room, home, or counseling appointment, "Lord, please allow me to represent you well. Take my hands, my lips, my words and use them to minister to this person." I carry on my key chain a small stainless steel vial of anointing oil (this can be ordered from your local Cokesbury store or other Christian bookstore). I have found it meaningful to

> The pastor's role in hospital calling and ministry with the sick is in many ways as important as—if not (at times) more important than— that of the physician.

use the oil to make the sign of the Cross on the individual's forehead as I pray for her, reminding her first of James 5:14-15, "Are any among you sick? They should call for the elders of the church and have them pray over them, anointing them with oil in the name of the Lord. The prayer of faith will save the sick."

I also carry a pocket-size New Testament and Psalms with me at all times, both for my use, and to use in the event I have the opportunity to share the scriptures with another. When making hospital calls I will try to have a scripture to share with the individual, a word of hope or comfort, before I enter the room.

I have found that the pastor's role in hospital calling and ministry with the sick is in many ways as important as—if not (at times) more important than—that of the physician. A pastor's role in caring for the sick is to dispense hope, comfort, and peace. Good physicians can provide a degree of this. But the pastor provides this like no one else can, for the pastor embodies and represents the presence of Christ, and draws upon the promises of the gospel in providing care.

The mind-body connection is profound. Our brain is our "central processing unit" and it has a great deal of control over our physical well-being, our response to illness, and our experience of pain. The human spirit, whether one locates this within the brain or apart from it, has the potential to influence the brain's thought patterns and the processes that are controlled by it. Most of us have been with someone who had given up on life, losing all hope, and within a matter of days the person died. The doctors can find no physiological reason why the person should have expired; the reason was primarily psychological, emotional, or spiritual. On the other hand, I have ministered with many people, who, in the face of a terrible illness, far outlived their physicians' estimates of life expectancy. Sometimes these people lived years longer than expected or they saw miraculous healing take place in their bodies that is medically unexplainable. But their bodies' ability to fight can only be explained in light of their faith, hope, and will to live.

There are literally hundreds of stories from my own ministry that have led me to the conclusion that faith plays a significant part in one's physical healing. One parishioner I visited was strapped to her hospital bed, hallucinating and experiencing severe depression that resulted from an extended and unidentifiable illness. When I entered her hospital room and began to talk with her and pray with her she calmed down. As I read the psalms aloud to her there was peace, and this marked the beginning of her turnaround. Another parishioner was near death. I administered Holy Communion to him and reminded him of the hope he had in Christ by telling him stories of parishioners who had had near-death experiences, stories that would help him trust in the hope Christ promises us. When I entered his hospital room you could sense the anxiety flowing from him. The doctors and nurses were not equipped to help him die. But when I left that night there was a palpable sense of the "peace that passes understanding" that would continue to guard his mind during the next few days until Christ, the Good Shepherd, welcomed him home.

Is Pastoral Care Exclusively the Senior Pastor's Job?

As much as I enjoy caring for my flock and offering pastoral care, I have, at several times in my ministry, been so overwhelmed with pastoral care that I had no time left to prepare quality sermons, lead the staff, spiritually feed myself, or seek God's vision for the church. The entire church suffered because I was trying to be "Super Pastor" by giving pastoral care to all who had need.

My family also suffered as a result of my misguided attempts at trying to fulfill this role. I would spend night after night at appointments in the evening, missing my children's activities because someone was in crisis. Regardless of how much time I committed to ministering to individuals in our congregation, there was never enough time and I found I was constantly falling short by failing to call upon someone or to go see someone I knew was in need. Every weekend when we would come to the prayer of confession in the worship service my prayer was the same, "Lord, forgive me for being such a failure as a pastor!" The guilt, both from my failure as a father and my failure as a pastor, was debilitating. I eventually realized that this could not continue. Something had to change.

Two things did change that helped restore balance for me: First, I began to realize that in most situations individuals could wait twenty-four to forty-eight hours to see a pastor, and just as they schedule appointments during the day to see the doctor, they could schedule appointments during the day to see me. (There are obvious exceptions to this rule that require immediate pastoral care, such as potential suicides or domestic violence, but most situations in which I have ministered could have waited until the next day for me to become involved.) When I offered to meet with persons calling me within the next few days, and then offered to pray with them by phone, they generally seemed relieved and grateful for my care, and were willing to wait, understanding I was unavailable at that moment. This allowed me to gain some control over what needed to be my family time.

The second change was when we as a church began to entrust pastoral care to others besides me. This started when we hired a staff member who began assisting with pastoral care as well as several other key ministry areas. Though he was not ordained, our congregation received him as one of its pastors. Later we added other ordained pastors to our staff who took on the lion's share of pastoral care. This was a critical step for the church, and for me. But the most important step in helping the church provide adequate pastoral care, while freeing the church's dependence on me for this vital ministry, was when we began to train laypeople to be a part of our pastoral team. We currently have a team of Stephen Ministers and a team of lay hospital callers who provide much of the pastoral care for our church family.

The most important step in helping the church provide adequate pastoral care was when we began to train laypeople to be a part of our pastoral team.

The Stephen Ministry is a wonderful program in which laypersons are trained in providing Christian care. When members of our congregation need ongoing ministry and encouragement, we connect them with one of these caregivers. The Stephen Minister will meet with them daily or weekly as needed. These caregivers stand by congregation members, listen to them, pray with them, and offer encouragement and hope. It would be impossible for one of our ordained pastors to spend this quantity of time with parishioners on a regular basis. But Stephen Ministers, because they are generally only assigned one or two care receivers at a time, can devote this kind of attention to the parishioner. The response of our laity who have been care receivers has been magnificent. They are so appreciative of this important ministry. (The Stephen Ministries is an organization located in St. Louis, Missouri. It offers training opportunities for volunteer caregivers in many churches and denominations throughout the world. Its website is *www.stephenministries.com.*)

Likewise our lay hospital callers do an incredible job. They visit the hospitals daily. Our goal, though not always achieved, is that every participant in our church who is hospitalized for an extended stay will have three to five visits per week from laity or clergy, most of these by our lay hospital callers. We work to teach our congregation that these callers represent Christ and the church, and we let our congregants know about this program before they join, so they are aware that hospital calling will be done by both laity and clergy.

I would reiterate that this idea of mobilizing laity for pastoral ministry is biblical. The idea goes back as far as Moses, who appointed others (laity) among the Israelites to judge between the cases being brought to him, so he could do the work of leading (see Exodus 18:17-26). It is seen in a powerful way in the early church's appointment of Stephen, Philip, and the other deacons to care for the physical needs of the Hellenistic converts, as seen in Acts 6:1-6:

> Now during those days, when the disciples were increasing in number, the Hellenists complained against the Hebrews because their widows were being neglected in the daily distribution of food. And the twelve called together the whole community of the disciples and said, "It is not right that we should neglect the word of God in order to wait on tables. Therefore, friends, select from among yourselves seven men of good standing, full of the Spirit and of wisdom, whom we may appoint to this task, while we, for our part, will devote ourselves to prayer and to serving the word." What they said

pleased the whole community, and they chose Stephen, a man full of faith and the Holy Spirit, together with Philip, Prochorus, Nicanor, Timon, Parmenas, and Nicolaus, a proselyte of Antioch. They had these men stand before the apostles, who prayed and laid their hands on them.

God did amazing things through these "lay" ministers who were commissioned and set aside to assist the apostles in their work. And the result of this effort was that "the word of God continued to spread; the number of the disciples increased greatly in Jerusalem" (Acts 6:7).

Ensuring that excellent pastoral care is provided to the congregation is the responsibility of the senior pastor, but all of this care need not be done directly by the pastor. The pastor's job is to ensure that the systems and people are in place to provide this care. In fact, in Ephesians 4:11-12 we read, "The gifts he gave were that some would be apostles, some prophets, some evangelists, some pastors and teachers, *to equip the saints for the work of ministry*, for building up the body of Christ" (emphasis added). Our task as leaders in the church isn't to do all of the work of the ministry, but to equip the saints to do the work of the ministry. When church leaders begin to understand this, the ministry of the church is able to explode. But when the church sees its senior pastor as the sole caregiver in the congregation, the church will always be limited in the kind, quality, and quantity of healing and care it can offer, and the pastor will always struggle with the guilt of not ever doing quite enough.

As our church has continued to grow I do less and less direct pastoral care. I still am involved in this area with occasional hospital calls, funerals, weddings, and pastoral counseling, but this is now more for my benefit than for others. I find that I must stay connected to the needs and hurts of people in our congregation. I must remember what our congregants real-life experiences are in order to lead our congregation. But most of the pastoral care I offer is through others. My job as senior pastor is both to make sure that we have the staff, systems, programs, and people in place to offer great pastoral care and also to provide sermons that address the pastoral care needs of the congregation. And finally it is through offering both visionary leadership and clear expectations to our staff and laity regarding pastoral care that I help our leaders to provide the pastoral care our congregation needs.

The Difference Between Small Churches and Large Churches

One of the critical differences between the large church and the small church is the ability of the senior pastor to provide one-on-one care for each parishioner. Many small membership church pastors act as chaplains for their congregations. The pastor visits in each home every year, is with every parishioner at times of surgery, is available for pastoral care over a cup of coffee whenever there is a need. This is often a blessing both for the pastor and the congregation in a small church. If you are in such a setting the only key change that a pastor or congregation might consider is developing lay leaders who will join the pastor in offering care, so that the pastor is able to focus on the important business of preparing excellent sermons

However, keep in mind that if your church is in an area with growth potential, this form of pastoral care will inhibit growth. It is difficult to maintain the chaplaincy model of ministry much beyond a weekly worship attendance of one hundred. This model will experience repeated failure when there are two hundred per weekend in worship. By the time you achieve three hundred per weekend in worship the senior pastor will experience constant frustration, guilt, and anxiety related to her or his inability to fulfill the responsibilities of the job of chaplain.

Some churches hire other staff to take over various functions of the church and want the senior pastor to preach and to continue to be available to offer pastoral care. Unfortunately this arrangement will spell doom for the church, for a pastor cannot provide the quality of leadership necessary to take the church into the future if he or she continues to be the primary caregiver of the congregation. Part of the reason is simple logistics. Parishioners cannot schedule their crises around the pastor's important meetings, sermon writing, and vision and strategic planning time. If the pastor is expected to be the primary pastoral caregiver then sermon writing, leading staff, and strategic planning will come up short.

One pastor I know was at the helm of a church with more than four hundred in worship every weekend. He had a great love for pastoral care and he was known for the remarkable lengths he would go to in ministering to his flock. People told stories of him sitting with families in the waiting room for five or six hours while their loved ones were in surgery. He would take the entire day to drive to a neighboring town to attend the funeral of a grandparent or a cousin of a parishioner. His care was legendary. But his congregation and staff were underled and the church suffered under this kind of leadership. While he was pursuing pastoral care like this, there was no time left for leading the staff, strategic planning, or researching and writing excellent sermons. The church operated at a fraction of its true potential and this ultimately resulted in financial difficulties for the church, morale difficulties among the staff, and an inability to attract many of the thousands of new residents who were moving into the area.

Too many mainline congregations have chosen the chaplaincy model for the work of their senior pastors and the results have been similar to what I've just described. Pastors must value excellent pastoral care and develop the people and systems to ensure this is being offered. Pastors of smaller churches can do more of the pastoral care themselves than can pastors of growing or larger churches. All pastors must offer some pastoral care directly in order to remain in touch with people's needs. But if pastors devote an inordinate amount of time to pastoral care to the detriment of their sermon preparation, strategic planning, and leadership work, the quality of their ministries, and the health and vitality of their congregations will suffer.

Pastoral Care at Church of the Resurrection

It may be helpful to offer a picture of what pastoral care currently looks like at Church of the Resurrection. At this time we have sixty-five hundred full members, twenty-five hundred preparatory members (children at sixth-grade level and lower) and more than one thousand regular visitors. Our worship attendance averages between five thousand and six thousand per weekend. We currently employ two ordained pastors whose full-time work is in pastoral care. In addition they have one full-time administrative support person who handles all pastoral care telephone calls, takes care of scheduling, and processes data regarding pastoral care needs in the church. We have two additional pastors who are available as needed to help with the occasional overflow of pastoral care needs. This number of pastors seems very small for a congregation of nearly ten thousand people. But it works because of the large number of laity involved in pastoral care.

We currently have more than forty trained Stephen Ministers and more than twenty trained lay hospital callers. We also have a pager that we send home each night with one of our pastors so that someone is available twenty-four hours a day. We have two part-time nonordained counselors on staff who work five to ten hours per week overseeing our support group ministry, which consists of marriage enrichment, grief support, job loss support, miscarriage, infertility and pregnancy loss support, Alcoholics Anonymous, Overcomers Outreach, and many others. In addition, we have a team of more than one hundred laypeople who form our Calling Caring Network. Each of these persons is assigned twenty to thirty households in our church whom they call several times a year just to pray for them and see how they are doing.

Our prayer ministry is an important component of our pastoral care ministry. We have one staff person who devotes thirty hours per week to this ministry, and a part-time administrative assistant to support her work. We have a host of laity on the prayer team who pray over the intercessory prayer cards that are turned in each weekend (over one hundred per weekend). Our pastors pray over every intercessory prayer request card, and our staff prays over them as well during our weekly staff chapel service. We have a weekly Service of Prayer and Healing at which communion is served and those who desire individual prayer accompanied by anointing with oil may receive this blessing. Here too we have laity who are a part of this ministry. One of our pastors leads the service and consecrates the Communion elements, but our laity join the pastors at the altar to pray for the sick. Often congregation members will approach one of our laity who is offering prayer at this service before they will one of the pastors because they have a particular relationship with the layperson or have come to experience this person's compassionate care in prior services. In addition to our pastors and laity, our staff members are expected to offer pastoral care for the volunteers or the participants in their ministry areas. Some of our finest caregivers on the staff are our administrative assistants and receptionists who understand that their primary job is ministry to the people who call or stop by.

Finally, much of the care that takes place in our church today is offered by church members to one another through our small groups including Sunday school classes, committees, ministry teams, and our Bible study groups.

In addition to the many pastoral care opportunities I've covered in this chapter, there are two special opportunities for pastoral care that warrant extra attention, weddings and funerals, to which I will now turn my attention.

ELEVEN

Weddings and Funerals

Weddings

Weddings are tremendous opportunities for both pastoral care and evangelism. I know of pastors who dread doing weddings, especially for persons who are not members of their churches. I understand this. A wedding represents a significant investment of time including evenings and weekends. But I feel weddings are one of the most remarkable opportunities to reach people for Christ and to help give spiritual direction for a family for generations to come.

For the first ten years of my ministry I would meet three to four times with couples preparing for marriage. At first I did this in the evenings. Later I came to understand that couples were taking time off from work to meet with florists, photographers, and caterers and that they could and would do the same to meet with the pastor. I began scheduling premarital counseling sessions at 4:00 P.M. on certain days of the week.

During our sessions together I would try to get to know the couple. I would ask them to tell me their stories—how they fell in love, why they want to marry, and the stories of their family of origin. We would also spend time discussing each of the following five topics: communication and fighting fairly, finances and budgeting, extended family and children, sexual intimacy and affair proofing a marriage, and finally, the Christian view of marriage and the role spirituality plays in making a great marriage. In each session we would cover two of these topics. In the process of their sharing stories about their lives, and me sharing stories from my marriage and life, we would come to know one another very well. I would end each session with prayer, joining hands with them and praying for God's blessings on each of them. In our last session together I would help them understand how a strong Christian faith can make all the difference in the quality of a marriage, and I would share with them concrete examples from my own marriage. I would also invite them to consider becoming Christians and joining the church if they were not already active in their faith. By the time we prayed our last prayer together at the end of our counseling, I had, in fact, become their pastor and I had spoken with them about things no one else would have felt comfortable talking about. A very high percentage of these couples ultimately joined our church and became committed Christians.

When I officiate at a wedding my aim is to do so with excellence. This starts with the rehearsal. I have a standard template for my wedding ceremonies on my computer. I change out the names and special music but otherwise it remains about the same from wedding to wedding. At our last counseling session I go over the ceremony with the couple and make any final changes. I ask that couples arrive with their guests fifteen minutes before the wedding rehearsal.

The trustees require that all rehearsals begin at 5:00 P.M. on the night before the wedding so that the pastors can have the remainder of the evening with their families. Seldom do I attend rehearsal dinners because of the number of evenings I am already away from home. By having the rehearsal at 5:00 P.M., a pastor can be home with his family by 6:00 P.M. (In smaller churches, the rehearsal dinner may be an important pastoral care opportunity that the pastor should attend. But as the church grows and the pastor's evening commitments grow, this is one place where the pastor may graciously step back.)

At the rehearsal we have a wedding coordinator who sets the sanctuary up for the wedding and who unlocks the church and helps the bridal party get ready. She is paid by the couple for her services. (Our coordinators are laity at Church of the Resurrection who lead this ministry!) This helps the wedding go much more smoothly and again saves the pastor from having to be at the church hours ahead of time setting things up. I begin each wedding rehearsal with prayer for the couple, then I try to build rapport with the bridal party. I give clear direction for the rehearsal, which allows for a better experience. (I have assisted pastors who do not do this, and these rehearsals take twice as long and can create frustration for the bride or groom when there is no one clearly in charge.)

On the wedding day I arrive thirty minutes before the wedding and check in on the bride and groom. I pray with the groom and his groomsmen

> **When I officiate at a wedding my aim is to do so with excellence.**

five minutes before the wedding begins. Our wedding ceremony is directly out of *The Book of Worship of The United Methodist Church,* with a few small modifications. I always offer an eight to ten minute message at every wedding. I begin each homily by sharing information about the couple. I tell how they met, why they fell in love, including a humorous story they have shared with me. Then I will briefly mention the things they have told me about each other—what it is they love and treasure about the other. (During premarital counseling I ask them to write me a letter describing these things, and in addition I invite them to share them with me verbally during the session. I let them know up front that I will use some of this information in the wedding service.) This makes the wedding very personal. Following this I briefly describe the biblical ideal of Christian marriage. I speak about marriage as a ministry, a sacred calling from God. In marriage a man accepts from God the calling to love, encourage, and minister to his wife. Likewise the woman accepts the same calling toward her husband. I use the story of the creation of Adam and Eve and describe the calling there—that Adam and Eve were to be helpers and companions to each other. I almost always share the scripture from Colossians 3:12-17, which I see as a powerful recipe for a wonderful marriage. I then will tell a story of how I have seen this ministry of marriage lived out by someone at the edge of life, either an elderly couple in our church who still love each other deeply, or a spouse who cares for her mate while he is ill, or one of a dozen other stories from parishioners who have effectively lived out the marriage covenant. The goal is not only to speak to the couple, but to speak to the congregation, and to teach them and witness to them regarding the value of faith in the context of marriage.

We have had hundreds of people who have joined our church who indicate that the first time they ever visited was at one of our weddings. A wedding, done well, not only blesses the bride and groom, but is an opportunity to reach guests who may not have been in church in years. Likewise, a wedding done poorly, will reinforce for these same people all of the reasons they do not attend church.

Recently I attended a wedding at another mainline church here in Kansas City. The family members were nominally involved in the church. The wedding processional took longer than the wedding ceremony. The pastor shared nothing personal about the couple. He had no homily. He seemed simply to have plugged the names of the bride and groom into his wedding ceremony without giving any thought to this couple or the people in the congregation. The entire wedding was finished, from processional to recessional, in fifteen minutes. It was the most dissatisfying and disappointing experience I had had in a church in a long time. Not only did the bride and groom need a pastor and a church since neither attended one, many of the guests also needed a church. But the service only served to reiterate for those present that the church is irrelevant.

One last word concerning wedding fees. We charge a standard sanctuary use fee, a custodial fee, a wedding coordinator's fee, an organist's fee, a fee for the sound and light operator, and a fee for the pastor. We have tried to keep these fees as low as possible. There is no difference in these fees between a member or a nonmember, hence there is no reason for someone to join the church just to get a discount on her wedding. But what we do offer for our members and visitors is the opportunity to allow one's offerings made prior to the wedding apply toward the cost of the sanctuary fee, which in essence eliminates this part of the fee for most members. We also ask couples to worship with us at least three times before scheduling a wedding with us. Some churches may wish to completely underwrite most of the wedding fees in order to encourage nonmembers to marry in their buildings. At the same time there needs to be a suggested honorarium for the pastor and some fee that is set for the church. The reason for this is, in part, because our society values things based upon their cost, and will sometimes not see the value in something that is free.

At Church of the Resurrection weddings can be booked no more than twelve months out, and a pastor is not assigned until six months out. I conduct about one-third of the weddings at Church of the Resurrection today, about ten to twelve per year. Our other pastors conduct the remaining weddings.

Funerals

Few opportunities are filled with more potential for a pastor and an entire congregation to represent Christ in reaching out to hurting and often nonreligious people than the funeral. As a young pastor I jumped at the opportunity to do a funeral for a family who did not have a church home, knowing that every time the funeral home called, I had the opportunity to minister to lost

> The visit a day or two before the funeral is designed to help family members grieve, remember, and celebrate.

sheep at a time of great need. Quality pastoral care at times of death always includes going to the home of the deceased or his family. When I minister with a member who is near death, I will make every effort to be with the family members and to pray with them one last time before death. If I do not have the opportunity to do this, I will go to the family's home as soon as possible following the death of the loved one.

Once there I will be sparse with my words, offering instead Christ's presence. I will share scriptures related to our hope in Christ. I will offer a prayer, inviting the entire family to join hands. During this prayer we commend the deceased to the Lord while inviting the Holy Spirit to offer comfort to the family. I will help the family think through its plans for burial. And then I will set up another time to come by to actually plan the funeral service. I suggest the family invite to this second visit those who were closest to the deceased. If I did not have the opportunity to minister with the family before the death, the visit for planning the funeral is the only visit I may have with the family. A day or two before the funeral, I will sit down with the family, explain a bit about the funeral service itself, and then begin asking leading questions concerning the deceased.

My goal is to learn as much as possible about the loved one. I find that this time of sharing is an important part of my ministry to the family. This visit will take about an hour, but it is designed not simply to help me put the funeral together, but to help family members grieve, remember, and celebrate. By the time I leave, healing has already begun. I pray for the family one last time and then depart. I always ask if I may take a photo of the deceased with me so that as I am preparing the funeral service I can look at the individual and reflect on what I've learned about his life. When I leave the family's home I typically have ten to fifteen pages of notes about the deceased person's life. These all help me in crafting a well-written eulogy.

At the funeral my aim is to speak on behalf of the family members in telling the story of their loved one and celebrating the individual's life. I typically will unite the eulogy and homily, beginning with the retelling of the deceased's life, replete with stories and personal anecdotes from the family. If I did not know the individual I will acknowledge this up front by saying, "I did not know your loved one, but I would like to share with you the memories and reflections of his closest family members."

I encourage family members to allow me to take the lead in sharing their loved one's story rather than having others speak. Generally the family is glad not to have anyone else share if I explain why this may be best. I am gentle in making this suggestion, leaving open the possibility of allowing others to speak, but clearly trying to steer away from this. If the family wants others to share, I ask that the persons sharing write down their remarks and give them to me before the funeral, preferably the day before. This allows me to craft my words around what the guests say. In addition, it helps ensure that the individual keeps her comments to the point. Some of the most painful and unhelpful funerals I have attended were those where the officiating pastors allowed a microphone to be passed around or invited a number of guests to speak. Often those speaking do not understand what is helpful and what is hurtful at funerals. They sometimes feel compelled to make theological statements that are uninformed and often reinforce inadequate views of God for those present. And occasionally their comments wander, or they break down emotionally, which creates a tone for the service that does not promote the beginning of healing.

The pastor should be the expert in helping the family plan the funeral. His or her aim is to help the family avoid a funeral that will be embarrassing, painful, or unhelpful. The average family has planned only one or two funerals. Family members simply do not have the experience to know what is helpful and what is not. The pastor's aim must be, in part, to help the family share in a funeral that will honor the deceased while bringing comfort to the living.

When it comes to the rest of the service, I will invite suggestions for songs for the funeral, but I may also make suggestions based upon the stories the family has shared with me. Again I find that most families do not have enough experience planning funerals nor do they know enough quality funeral music to be able to suggest something that might be perfect. They typically will suggest the two or three songs most people are familiar with: "Amazing Grace," "How Great Thou Art," and "In the Garden." If I have an opportunity to spend several hours reflecting on the life stories of the deceased, I may find that another hymn or some other special song may better fit the direction the service will take, and thus I will often ask for permission to choose or suggest special music.

> **The homily must be real, genuine, and reflect integrity with the actual life experiences of those who knew the deceased.**

This is true of the scripture passages to be read as well. Unless the family has strong feelings, I will ask permission to spend time praying about and reflecting on the loved one's life and then, based upon this, select scriptures that seem to fit the loved one's story and which will tie into the rest of the service. The pastor's role in designing the funeral is to weave all of the elements together into a helpful, healing, and cohesive whole. A key point of the service is the eulogy/homily. My aim is to establish this as one unit, to tell the deceased's story and then to seamlessly move into the proclamation of the gospel.

I have found that the homilies offering the most healing were not simply sugarcoated promises of eternal life. No, the homily must be real, genuine, and reflect integrity with the actual life experiences of those who knew the deceased. One woman whose father had passed away told me at her home, "I hated my father. There was nothing good about him at all." Her tears betrayed a great deal of pain. I could not simply ignore this at the funeral. At the same time it had to be handled carefully as he had other family members who did not feel this way. That service was an opportunity to care for this family and to help it make sense of this man without dismissing the pain many felt.

Suicides are challenging for this same reason. The pastor cannot simply ignore the form of death, even though the family may often wish him or her to do so. I always ask for permission to try to bring something good from the loved one's death by referring to the suicide in order to help others see why this was not the right path to choose. At the same time I try to help the family and friends understand God's grace toward the deceased.

One funeral I performed was for a woman who had died as a result of drinking and driving. She was a relatively young woman and completely nonreligious. The same was true for her family and friends. I took seriously their stories and avoided being "overly religious" at the family's request. At the same time I gently opened the door to faith questions by asking, at her memorial, "I have been wrestling, as I prepared this service, with this question, 'What would G—— want to say to you, her friends, now that she is gone?' " You could hear a pin drop in the funeral home chapel. It was in response to this question that I was able to broach her tragic death, a life cut short. I was able to allow her to speak to her friends about not being reckless or taking life for granted. And finally, I spoke of the meaning of life, and God the giver of life. I raised the possibility that God had more in store for her life than this, and that the great tragedy would be for her death to have counted for nothing. I helped the mourners see that we will all face death one day. The questions will be, "What did we do with our lives?" and "What did we hope for in our deaths?" Then I gently offered them words of hope from the gospel. What was a terrible tragedy took on meaning and, at least for some who were present, was a time in which their hearts were turned toward God.

I recently attended two funeral services as a friend of the family, services where other pastors presided. In one an associate pastor presided. He was not particularly charismatic in his presentation, and the service itself was not well crafted. But he shared a meaningful eulogy/homily that was faithful to the hope of the gospel while sharing personal and humorous anecdotes about the deceased. It was wonderfully healing for the family.

Several weeks before this I had attended another funeral, for a man who sometimes attended our church, but whose membership was elsewhere. The pastor who presided was a prominent pastor in the area. The sanctuary was beautifully decorated. The order of service was actually better crafted than most. But the pastor's eulogy so missed the mark. It was delivered stiffly, without warmth, humor, or any evidence that the pastor had spent much time with the family. It was a recounting of the facts of the person's life without telling his story. The homily was cold, a barely warmed-over version of the same homily this man must have preached a hundred times before. The entire service was over in seventeen minutes. You could feel the aching hearts of the family and friends after the service. The difference between the two services was the time the pastor spent with the family, his willingness to take the time to honor the deceased and to really tell his story, and the effort one pastor put into developing a homily based upon the individual's life versus offering a standard funeral message that had been preached a hundred times before.

A good funeral will take at least ten hours on the part of the pastor to visit with the family, pray, to craft the service and homily, to rehearse the message (yes, even the best preachers do well to rehearse the message at least once ahead of time), to officiate, and then to spend time with the family following the service. On another note, I often officiate the funeral services at our church or a local funeral home and, if the interment is at a local cemetery, I will officiate there as well. But if the burial is some distance away it is possible that one of our associate pastors may do the interment, or possibly a pastor from that local community will officiate if the family has a church home there. I mention this for those who pastor larger churches; it is not always possible to devote fifteen to twenty hours a week to one service, which is what will be required if the interment is two or more hours away. There are alternatives to this which, when the appropriate introductions with other pastors are made, will make it possible to turn over the interment to someone else.

As was the case with weddings, we have had hundreds of people who first began attending Church of the Resurrection at a funeral and who eventually became members. Every funeral is filled with a large number of people who may not darken the door of a church at any other time. And they are wrestling with truly important questions about death, the meaning and purpose of life, how we understand God's role in relationship to evil and suffering, and so much more. A well-led funeral can move persons to want to reconnect with God and to visit your church. The key is in spending time with the family and then taking the time to develop a quality, meaningful ministry experience at the funeral.

TWELVE

Troubled Waters: Dealing with Opposition

It has been said that the most challenging part of leadership is dealing with those who oppose and sometimes actively undermine your leadership. Beth Fowler notes in a July 1997 article in *Supervision* journal that "if you can't remember the last time you were criticized then you're playing it too safe and missing out on opportunities for improvement." If you are unwilling to accept and stand in the face of criticism you may be in the wrong line of work, for pastors and church leaders who avoid criticism and conflict will never help a church reach its full potential.

It should be noted from the start that criticism can be very important. The critic may have a good point that you have not considered. It is possible that God has prompted his heart to speak up to keep you from making a terrible mistake. Sometimes those who criticize do so for all the right reasons. Your task as a leader is to be teachable and willing to listen to truly constructive criticism.

At the same time, leaders will also face a significant share of criticism that is neither constructive nor helpful. Knowing the reasons for such criticism, and how to respond to it, is critical if you ever hope to lead your church to become a dynamic congregation. Let me begin by acknowledging that good church people can be amazingly critical. There are several reasons for this. The first and most common reason for criticism and opposition to genuine leadership is our innate resistance to change.

The first and most common reason for criticism and opposition to genuine leadership is our innate resistance to change.

Most people fear change. We will be more critical of potential change than nearly anything else. This is true of small changes—the color of the carpet, the decor in the nursery, the times of the worship services. But the more significant the changes the more you should expect criticism and opposition. Good leaders expect this. They prepare for it and look for ways to help vocal critics feel an investment in the process early on, or they anticipate the criticism and address it before it takes place.

Several years ago we prepared to move into our second-phase sanctuary, a building that one day will be our fellowship hall. We were moving from a beautiful five hundred-seat room complete with Gothic arches and skylights. We were moving into a sixteen hundred-seat fellowship hall with no arches. We tried to anticipate, before moving into the room, the likely criticisms and concerns of our congregants. We knew that even our most attended service would fill only half of this new sanctuary, and that we would certainly not need the four hundred-seat balcony. We anticipated that some would criticize the fact that we built such a large room. Yet at the rate we were growing we knew we would need this space within a year. So two weeks before moving into the new sanctuary we addressed this issue head-on in a service, when we said, "As we prepare to move into the new sanctuary some of you will no doubt wonder why we built such a large room. After all we won't even use the balcony for the first twelve months. But every time you look at the empty seats in the balcony understand that those seats are for people whose names we don't know yet, who will meet Christ here. And be grateful that you had a building committee that was visionary enough to see not our current need, but what we will need a year from now." In less than a year we were seating people in the balcony and two years later we were completely filling the entire room at our lead service.

I could give example after example of this. Great leaders anticipate the criticism of their critics and address these beforehand. These leaders also recognize that criticism and opposition are to be expected if you are leading people into the future and into change. People are not bad because they oppose the changes you suggest; they are just being people. People resist change. Your task as a leader is to discern how to help them through this change and to rise above their fears and concerns, and to be willing to accept criticism as part of the price that must be paid for leading people to do what is best.

A second reason behind criticism stems from a failure to adequately communicate the reasons for the plan, proposal, vision, or change you seek to implement. I have often found that people criticize what they do not understand. If they do not understand it is either because they were not listening, or we as leaders did not adequately explain what we were doing. Communication is a critical part of leadership.

When you are leading a congregation to do ministry differently than in the past, or launching new ministries, or otherwise moving a congregation to embrace change, it will be essential that you overcommunicate. The larger the congregation the more communication will be necessary. People may not read their newsletters, may not be present on the Sunday when you unveil your plans in worship, or they may be present but not completely understand what you are proposing. It is critical that you communicate again and again and again.

People need to understand, first, the reason for the change, vision, or new ministry, and how this proposed change ties back to the purpose of the church and biblical ministry. This is the first and most important element that must be communicated. People will need to be reminded again and again of the biblical, theological, or missional reasons behind what you are proposing. Second, they need to understand exactly what you are proposing: What will this look like? Third, they need to understand clearly that you have considered the alternatives and the reasons you think this particular plan is the best. Fourth, they need to understand the implications of the proposal—the costs, the timing, and how it will affect them. Fifth, they need to see clearly the payoff or the reward. This is often a reminder of the reason for the change, but it offers a concrete picture of what the future will look like when the change, ministry, or vision is implemented. Finally, it is helpful if they can hear from respected leaders in the church who support what is being proposed.

Even when you have communicated these things well, you may still have persons who are resistant to the change you are proposing. Last year I had one of my key leaders say, "I still don't like this project that you have proposed, but I understand the need and I can't come up with a better plan. So, while I am not vocally supportive because of my reservations, I cannot actively oppose it either because I have no alternatives to offer." Sometimes that is the best you can expect as you lead others. But such a statement makes clear that you effectively communicated the need for the change, the payoff, and the costs, even if the plan you've proposed isn't enthusiastically embraced.

The truth is sometimes you will propose things that no one will be enthusiastic about, but about which there will be general agreement that it is the right thing to do. Few people get excited about having a root canal, and most approach the procedure with anxiety and reservations, but they do know that it is essential and they have no alternatives to offer.

The third and most challenging criticism leaders have to deal with is that which springs from personal issues on the part of the critic. These may be a result of the individual's desire to hold or gain power, her fear of losing control, her jealousy or a low self-esteem or both, some disappointment she experienced with your leadership in the past, or a personality conflict between her and you. These individuals are challenging to deal with because the real issue is not the plan or proposal you have made; the real issue is emotional, psychological, or relational.

Like a wounded animal, these persons can also be dangerous and hurtful. They tend to either act in a passive-aggressive way, appearing to be supportive of your leadership and concerned for you, while openly opposing you or working against you behind the scenes. Conversely, sometimes they are very vocal in their opposition and tend to be personal in their criticism. Many churches have been torn apart, and many pastors' ministries shipwrecked because of people like this. Know that you will experience this kind of opposition in your church; it is only a matter of time. There are a certain number of people like this in every church. They may get along wonderfully with many people, but for some reason their latent frustrations, wounds, or psychoses will be taken out on you. When this happens there are several important things to remember.

Remember that you are not alone. Every leader experiences this. Moses was criticized in the wilderness, David was nearly overthrown by his own son, Elijah was hated by King Ahab. Jesus had one of his inner circle, Judas, betray him and undermine his leadership. In the end, of course, our Lord was crucified by people who were threatened by his leadership. If you read the letters of Paul carefully it is apparent that he was opposed in nearly every town and not just by the pagans or the Jews, but by *Christians* in the churches. Throughout history the great leaders of the church have all experienced this—Augustine, Luther, Wesley. You are in good company! But there are some pointers I would offer that I have learned the hard way.

You cannot spend your entire ministry or large amounts of your emotional and spiritual energy focusing on the handful of people who will oppose your leadership.

First, do not blow things out of proportion. Usually we become obsessed with those who are opposing us, and sometimes we make their opposition out to be more than it really is. On occasion these folks weren't even that serious about their criticism, but we as leaders are hypersensitive and we let it consume us. Second, never stoop to their level. When you begin to publicly criticize others you undermine your own leadership. Third, find a trusted confidant that you can talk with, preferably outside of the church, to gain his honest feedback and assessment. I have found that my most vocal critics always spoke at least some truth and I can learn from them if I am willing to be teachable. But I need a third party to help me see this.

Fourth, know who the influencers are within your own congregation who will stand by you and stand up with you. Make sure they understand what is happening and enlist their help in either approaching the critic or in dispelling the criticism. (Ideally you would have a group in the church that would lend this support to you. In The United Methodist Church it is the staff-parish relations committee.) Fifth, approach these persons directly, early on, to hear their concerns. Do your best not to be defensive. Think over their concerns before responding. Perhaps plan on meeting a second time for a follow-up meeting at which you would like to be able to offer a prayerful and well thought out response. When you do this always look for points at which you can find common ground.

Sixth, if someone is consistently criticizing you and others, or if this person is consistently opposing needed changes or ministries, be cautious in where you allow him to exercise leadership. Some need to be kept from leadership positions altogether. Others should be used in leadership because they will offer valuable dissenting views, but should only be used on a team where you've got a strong leader who can compensate for their critical spirit. Otherwise, these persons will sidetrack any valuable ministry. Finally, do not respond to critics by E-mail. This is almost always a bad idea (something I've learned the hard way). It is so tempting to hit the "reply" button and to share, out of your frustration, anger, or hurt, your response. This response is almost never one that will serve you well, but now, in the hands of your critic, it can be freely forwarded to others who will not have the benefit of having the critic's original E-mail.

You cannot spend your entire ministry or large amounts of your emotional and spiritual energy focusing on the handful of people who will oppose your leadership. You must listen and try to learn from them. You must never forget that these are part of God's flock as well and that they earnestly believe what they are saying. You will not be able to make all people happy all of the time. There are some people for whom you are likely not the pastor who can best minister to them. The most helpful advice I have found in dealing with persons like this is from Jesus himself, who teaches us to pray for those who oppose us. Consider the good the individual raising this criticism believes she is trying to achieve. (Few people seek to oppose you simply because they want to do harm; they nearly always believe they are doing the right thing for the right reasons.) If you can see the issue from her perspective it will help you overcome your own negative feelings toward her. I have, at times, prayed for months on end for individuals, asking God to help me to love those who had hurt me. I have asked God to bless them and to help them move beyond that which has caused such action. And I have invited God to use them to help me to be the person God wants me to be. Again and again I have found that God is able to give me a love for persons who have hurt me, when I turn this over to him.

One last note relates to leadership as well as dealing with opposition. When it comes to important issues, don't leave their fate up to chance or the ability of a few opponents to successfully sidetrack them. I have never brought to a vote at our leadership team any important issue that I was not certain would be approved by a wide margin. By the time it comes up for a vote we have studied the options carefully, understanding all of the possible objections and developing answers to these or taking them into account in revising the proposal. We have got the key leaders completely on board and we have hinted at the plan and unveiled parts of it at previous leadership gatherings for two or three months prior to the vote. Finally, we try to ensure that our best presenters are making the proposals. Sometimes that will be me, but often it will be the chair of the ministry area making the proposal. Criticism and opposition can be painful. My wife and I have both been in tears in the past, and so discouraged that we were nearly ready to give up on our ministry. Remember that leaders will always face some opposition. Great ministries never happen apart from it. As a pastor or church leader you must expect criticism. Respond to it in a way that honors God and doesn't diminish your spiritual leadership. But whatever you do, do not allow the critics to keep your church from pursuing God's vision and mission.

THIRTEEN

Becoming a Visionary Leader

Vision is a key characteristic found in leaders who develop dynamic churches. It is usually lacking in pastors and church leaders who lead low-functioning churches. Some believe one is either born a visionary or not. They believe that one cannot learn how to be a visionary leader. I disagree. While I am certain that some people are naturally wired and gifted with vision, I am also persuaded that vision can be cultivated and learned. The aim of this chapter will be to make the case for visionary leadership and to offer concrete steps to improve your vision.

Within the local church the task of providing visionary leadership falls squarely on the pastor's shoulders. But the pastor is not alone in this task. According to the Scriptures the Holy Spirit works in our lives to give both young and old, clergy and laity, the ability to dream and vision:

'In the last days it will be, God declares,
that I will pour out my Spirit upon all flesh,
    and your sons and your daughters shall prophesy,
and your young men shall see visions,
    and your old men shall dream dreams.'
(Acts 2:17; see also Joel 2:28)

> The role of the visionary is to ask, "What do we need to do now in order to realize the best possible future for our congregation?"

At Church of the Resurrection, when we were just getting started in ministry, many of the visions and dreams for our ministry began with me. But today most of the dreams and visions for new ministry areas come from our laity, our ministry teams, or our staff. Yet when it comes to the overall vision of the church, and anticipating both potential problems and possible opportunities in the future, this responsibility still falls largely on my shoulders. In most large churches the senior pastor's job description will often include only three or four key tasks. Seeking God's vision for the church and providing visionary leadership is usually number two in the job description, second only to preaching, as a key expectation of these churches for their senior pastors. But what is vision? Vision is the ability to see possibilities, pitfalls, untapped potential, and a preferred picture of the future. Visionary leaders are like the nineteenth-century scouts who rode ahead of the wagon trains heading west along the Santa Fe Trail. The job of the scout was to be looking miles ahead to see where danger might lurk, or to find the shallow places to ford the rivers. Scouts would then come back to the wagon train and help it avoid peril and find opportunities for food, shelter, or improved paths.

The task of the pastor is to be the chief scout, with key lay leaders and other staff serving as a part of the scouting team, all of whom evaluate both the church's current situation and the future. You should be aware of the future possibilities and plans in your community. Will a new highway be built in your area in the next twenty years? Will your community likely become a bedroom community for a major city thirty miles away? Who is buying large amounts of land in the community and what do they plan to do with it? You should be in touch with what is happening in your local planning commission or city council, and your school system. It is possible, in some small towns, that you may be the most visionary leader in your town. Are you helping the town visualize a preferred picture of the future? Perhaps you see possibilities even the town leaders don't see yet. In addition, what do the growth trends and the demographics of your own congregation tell you about the future? If the average age of your congregation is sixty and those over fifty outnumber those under thirty five-to-one, it doesn't take a tremendous visionary to see that in twenty-five years the congregation will be a fraction of its current size, unless it reaches more young people.

The role of the visionary is not only to see the pitfalls and opportunities in the future, but to ask the question, "What does this mean for our church and what do we need to do now to realize the best possible future for our congregation in the years to come?" This is both rewarding and challenging. It requires taking a longer view than most pastors are willing to take. Many pastors are looking to the next three to five years, about the length of time they anticipate staying at their churches. Someone else can worry about the future. But visionary pastors are always concerned about the future, beyond the days when they will still be serving as pastor. And while the world is changing at a blinding speed, and the best long-range plans are subject to change, such planning must start somewhere.

It has been noted that many churches are hesitant to follow the long-term visions and dreams of a pastor, knowing that this pastor may only be with the church for a few years. This is one of the debilitating aspects of short tenures for local church pastors. The task of the pastor, in these situations, is to help the local church discover God's vision for the congregation. This vision transcends the tenure of a particular pastor. If the church needs to relocate to another side of town where more land and new development will help the church prosper during the coming decades, the goal must be to help the leaders of this congregation see that regardless of who the pastor may be, this is the right move. Furthermore, when the church and pastor are seeking *God's* will and vision for this church, as opposed to the senior pastor's vision, the congregation is more likely to move forward in pursuit of the vision regardless of how long the current pastor will stay at the helm.

Let's take a look at some real-life examples of concrete visions that I have helped our congregation identify and pursue in the last few years. Five years ago our church had experienced such tremendous growth that I knew that, based upon the growth projections of our community, we would run out of land within ten years. We owned a twenty-acre site, and at that time ten acres were under cultivation, not being used for the church at all. But seeing our growth trends, I was keenly aware that these ten acres of undeveloped ground would not sustain us in the future. There were another forty-five acres of land available for sale adjacent to our site. Because I was monitoring the future plans for land adjacent to the church I knew that the owner was developing plans to build apartments on these forty-five acres. Once the apartments were built the church would be hemmed in. When we did need more land, in ten years, it would no longer be available and the church would either need to relocate or choose to plateau and ultimately decline, unable to accommodate the likely demand placed upon it.

No one else in our church was thinking about this at that time. After all, we had ten acres of soybeans still awaiting development. And who in our church at that time could imagine that any church would need more than twenty acres of land? My lay leaders had not traveled to other large churches, the size we were likely to become, to know that none of them had as few as twenty acres, and that several had as many as one hundred acres. My task as senior pastor was to think about these things, to anticipate the future long-term needs of the church, to study other churches who are of the size we one day would become, to be aware of what is happening in the community, and then to alert our lay leadership in order to get them involved in the process. This is the pastor's job, just as it is the task of the leader of any organization, to be thinking of the future and be aware of the pitfalls and opportunities it may hold.

Ultimately I approached a small group of our lay leaders and began to ask them questions that would help them reach similar conclusions to those I had drawn about our long-term land needs. I invited them to project our future growth based upon demographic data I supplied from the county. I shared with them benchmarking data I had collected from other churches I had visited. In the end they agreed that we needed to acquire more land, and that the forty-five acres adjacent to our site was the right piece of property to target. From there this group took its conclusions to the administrative council of our church and led its members through the same discovery process. In the end our leadership voted to acquire the forty-five acres of land adjacent to the church (and since then we've acquired another forty-five acres adjacent to that tract) and authorized a team to begin negotiations for its purchase. But what would it take to convince a church that still had ten acres of undeveloped land that it needed to buy forty-five additional acres? It took a leader who was thinking about and scouting out the distant future, who was aware of the demographics of the community and the likely long-term growth potential of the church, and one who had benchmarked against other, larger churches to understand the real needs, concerns, and opportunities of these other congregations.

An interesting side note: within three years we had filled the entire ten acres that had been undeveloped on our site with parking and buildings. Within five years—not the ten I had originally projected—we were out of land altogether and working to expand parking onto the new land we had just purchased. Had I, as the pastor, not been doing my job in planning and scouting, it would have been three years before the congregational leaders might have realized we would need more land. And by that time apartments would have been constructed on that site, leaving us no option but to relocate.

Vision isn't just about future land needs, and it is not only about issues in the distant future. It is also about ministry today. Part of the task of the visionary leader is to seek God's vision for the congregation, across its ministry areas, and to encourage others to do the same. When we were a smaller church with few staff, I helped most of our major ministry areas to develop short- and medium-range visions. Today the staff and lay leaders of those ministry areas do that on their own. They do this not only with my encouragement, but also with my overall vision for the church and the growth projections and plans I've obtained for them to use in their decision making. Many pastors have asked me, "How do you develop visions for the church? What is the process? Is it something I can learn to do?"

> The problem behind our dwindling ranks has been a limited vision that permeates every level of leadership in our churches, which stems from a "safe" faith in an impotent God who no longer works in our world.

Fortunately, there is a process that can be defined, and most of
my visions for ministry have come from this process.

Ten Essential Ingredients for Developing and Implementing Visions in the Church

1. Prayer and Submission to Christ

As I discussed in chapter 2, we must always remember that
the pastor's primary responsibility is not to develop her or his
personal visions for the church. Neither is it to implement the
denomination's vision for the church. The primary task of the
pastor is to discern *God's* vision—God's preferred future—for
the congregation. If we really believe that the church belongs to
Christ, and that he has a plan for his church, then all vision must
begin with prayer coupled with a passionate desire to accomplish God's will. The discernment process that follows prayer
will be outlined in the following steps. The greatest and most
important visions in my ministry always came out of intense
times of prayer and yielding my life to Christ.

2. A Bold Faith and Trust in the Power of God

I love the title of J. B. Phillips's classic little book, *Your God Is
Too Small*. The title is an accurate assessment of the picture of
God that is held by many. Within the mainline denominations,
our primary struggle over the last thirty years has not been with
sociological phenomenon, lack of funding, or even the quality
of our candidates for ministry. The problem behind our dwin-
dling ranks has been a limited vision that permeates every level
of leadership in our churches, which stems from a "safe" faith
in an impotent God who no longer works in our world.

This is evident when denominational officials purchase a
five to ten acre church site in a community with tens of thousands of unchurched people, because they believe that
"churches in our denomination don't grow beyond one thou-

sand people in worship." This is what we were told by one expert in church planting when our leaders wanted to purchase a twenty-acre site in 1992. The expert recommended a five-acre site. When we asked where we would park all of the cars he offered a knowing smile, amused by the young pastor whose visions of thousands of people attending a United Methodist Church in Kansas was "completely beyond the realm of the possible!" Our consultant's vision was limited by what had happened in the past. He was right; historically, there were no churches that averaged more than one thousand in worship attendance in the Kansas East Conference of The United Methodist Church. But just because there had not been any in the past did not mean that there couldn't be any in the future! Too often nothing great happens in our churches because we have visions that are so small and don't take into account the power of God! Churches and leaders who have and achieve great visions always have a bold faith and trust in the power of God to do all things, in the words of the apostle Paul, "exceeding abundantly above all that we ask or think" (Eph. 3:20 KJV).

3. Assessing the Congregation

Once you've come to trust that God can do unbelievable things through willing people, it is time to assess the true potential of your congregation, a potential that is always much greater than members believe, but sometimes a bit less than a visionary pastor might hope for. I knew one pastor who had a vision of his congregation reaching thousands upon thousands of people, but the congregation was located in a community where there were only three thousand residents, and there were ten other churches all seeking to minister to them. The assessment of your congregation will require asking a lot of questions and honestly evaluating its strengths and weaknesses. Inviting an outside consultant to help with this process may offer insights not readily apparent to you or to the congregation's leaders. Among the questions you must ask are: What are the demographics of this congregation—age, stage in life, emotional, physical, and spiritual health, and economics? What is the untapped potential in human resources? What is your facility like? The location? The parking? In what ways is your facility being underutilized? How will your facility or location inhibit your ministry? How will it support it? Who are the potential leaders who might be willing to follow your leadership and vision?

4. Benchmarking

Sharp, creative, and visionary leaders are constantly looking for great ideas that they can adapt or port directly to their organization. They are continuously studying organizations that are "best in class" as well as those that are at the next tier up from themselves. Effective pastors and church leaders do the same thing. They study churches that are "best in class" in various ministry areas. These are often, but not always, churches that are very large. From these churches a pastor, staff member, or lay leadership team will gain new ideas for ministry as well as a broader vision of what is actually possible.

At Church of the Resurrection I have taken key staff or leaders on benchmarking trips numerous times. In our second year I was trying to cast a vision of the kind of church I thought we could become. But it wasn't until I took a team of six lay leaders and staff to a seminar at The United Methodist Church of the Servant in Oklahoma City in 1992 that my leaders were able to see what I had been seeing in my mind. That event was invaluable for me as well, because I was able to see my vision actually being lived out in another local church. It helped me see what the future could look like, gave me ideas on what I wanted to steer clear of, and what I wanted to emulate from that fine church. From that time on I have traveled to visit other large churches every year in my ministry, usually taking others along to catch a glimpse of where I thought we might be heading.

In 1998 our church had grown, in terms of worship attendance, beyond all of the other churches I had visited up to that time. I felt I needed to recharge my own batteries, to gain new insight into the uncharted territory that we were heading into, and to learn from larger-church pastors about the issues, struggles, and opportunities inherent in churches that achieved more than three thousand per weekend in worship. The church granted me a two-month sabbatical leave during which my family and I traveled thirteen thousand miles, most of it in a conversion van pulling a pop-up camper. That year we visited twenty-six of the largest churches in the United States. I met with staff members and pastors from these congregations, worshiping in many of them, examining their facilities, staffing, systems, history, and plans for the future.

When I came back from this trip I had forty-eight single-spaced typed pages of new ideas for ministries, or ways of improving ministries we already had in place. Few of these ideas were taken directly from the other churches, but all were inspired by my study of them. You may not be able to take a two-month sabbatical, but you can schedule one or two trips a year to visit the outstanding churches of America. Most host their own leadership schools annually. Do not restrict yourself to churches of your denomination or even churches of your own theological bent. Some of the most important insights and ideas for new ministries that I have gained over the years came from churches that were very different from my own theological perspectives.

> **Visionary leaders are continuously studying organizations that are "best in class," as well as successful organizations that are at the next tier up from themselves.**

In addition to studying the world-class churches, it is important that you also network with and study churches that are at the next tier up in size or scope of ministry from your church. Many church consultants suggest that one key to developing a dynamic church is to begin doing the things that churches the next tier up from yours are doing, and by implementing some of their systems and ways of doing ministry, your congregation will begin to live into that type of church. Benchmarking is crucial to the visioning process, for it opens up your own creativity as you seek God's vision for your church.

5. Surveying Unmet Needs, Underserved Constituencies, and Missed Opportunities

Critical to developing visions for your congregation is the process of looking for and analyzing the unmet needs within your congregation and the community, noting the underserved constituencies of people, and the missed opportunities that no one else in the community is capitalizing on. Let me give a few examples.

A church in a small town struggles to find a missional purpose and ministry outside of the walls of the church and thus begins to lose some of its vitality. Yet just outside of town is a prison facility filled with men who don't know Christ. What an opportunity! What if the pastor carefully studied the unrealized potential of the congregation—the men and women who worked in the prison, the influence this church had in the community, the number of members who could take time off during the day, and the number of members who were more mature in their faith (assessing the congregation)? What would happen if the pastor researched and studied those churches across America that were located near prisons, to see what they were doing in ministry to prisoners (benchmarking)? Finally what would happen if the pastor met with prison officials and inmates to determine what the unmet needs of prisoners and prison staff might be (surveying)? Suddenly a huge mission field opens up before this congregation; new opportunities to witness to the gospel present themselves. But none of this is likely to happen without a visionary leader who is willing to move a congregation outside of its comfort zone to do what is difficult in order to faithfully serve God.

In our own congregation we are constantly surveying the unmet needs, underserved constituencies, and missed opportunities in the community. And in response, we are continually launching new ministries to help us accomplish our mission of introducing people to Christ and providing life-transforming ministry. As I mentioned briefly in chapter 4, we noticed years ago that there were hundreds of new apartment units going up near the church. Demographics in our area indicate that a large percentage of the apartment residents are single adults in their thirties. The other churches offering strong singles programs were either more than ten miles from these apartments or they offered little for singles in their thirties. This represented a tremendous ministry opportunity. Having visited several churches with single-adult ministries that attracted thousands of singles, I had a picture in my mind of what this could look like. We made this a congregational priority, devoted funds to hire staff, developed Sunday school classes and weeknight programs, and then allocated funds for marketing. The results are promising. Already seven hundred singles have connected with our ministry and four new Sunday school classes have been formed just for singles. Brainstorm with community leaders and the leaders in your congregation so that your church can "see a need and meet it."

6. Time for Daydreaming

One thing is certain: it is difficult to hear God's voice or to discern God's vision unless you take time for this purpose. Most pastors are so focused on their day-to-day ministry that they are not able to clear their minds, pray, and listen. God speaks to us as God did to Elijah, through the "still small voice," but it is hard to hear that voice unless you are very quiet for prolonged periods of time. Your greatest visions will come when you've done all of the things listed above, and then taken the time—several hours a week, a two-day retreat once a month, a weeklong sabbatical each summer—just to seek God's vision for your church.

As I noted in the chapter on preaching, I take several silent retreats every year both to write sermons, but also to pray and seek God's vision. Every summer I take two weeks away for study, reflection, and discernment. I reflect on all of the things listed above, I pray, and I allow myself time to dream. By the time I come home I have no shortage of dreams and visions that

I feel are God inspired. Usually I have far too many to try to implement them all in the year or two to come. Every summer I make a list that begins with these words: "In five years I hope that Church of the Resurrection will. . . ." Some of the items from prior years get crossed off the list through the steps that follow this one. Most of these visions have become reality, or they have moved up higher on the list. Each year I set twelve to fifteen goals for my own ministry; these are visions that I will strive to pursue or sometimes visions that I will help another ministry area pursue. My aim is to have accomplished at least half of these in the year to come. I share these goals with our staff-parish relations committee (the lay committee that oversees personnel concerns) and use it to evaluate my performance with these goals at the end of the following year. Most of these visions, dreams, and goals would never have materialized were it not for taking the time away to pray, reflect, and listen for God's guidance.

7. Testing the Waters

As you begin to develop visions and dreams that you believe are God inspired, it is essential that you begin to test these visions, to share them with a handful of people whose judgment you trust, who believe in the mission of the church, and who have the kind of faith in God that knows that God is able to do great things through the church. Share your ideas, hopes, and plans with these persons. Ask them to pray about your visions and to offer their critique, their suggestions, their assessments, and their ideas. My wife, LaVon, is also my most trusted advisor on this front. I can't think of a single vision for ministry that I did not first discuss with her. Her wisdom and insight have been invaluable in saving me from

> Do not be discouraged by opposition. Listen and learn, but if you have strong support for the vision from a large number of your leaders, charge ahead.

pursuing foolish things, while encouraging me and helping to perfect visions that have helped the church become what it is today. Sharing these things with her has also served to strengthen our relationship and the sense that we are a team in a shared ministry.

After clarifying and revising these visions with LaVon I will then share them with those members of my lead staff who have the greatest vested interest in them, since many of these ideas affect their ministry areas. I ask for staff members' honest feedback and their insights. Again this leads to clarifying and revising these visions. Next I share these visions with several different groups of key lay leaders including our church council and our ministries council—two administrative groups providing leadership in the church. As I already mentioned, I share a written copy of my goals and visions with our staff-parish relations committee.

Finally, I share many of these visions with our laity at a special retreat each January to which all current or future leaders of the church are invited. Part of the purpose of this retreat is the opportunity for me to begin casting these visions to the congregation. At each of these steps the visions are becoming clarified, revised, and sometimes discarded.

Some of the visions that come out of this process are smaller in scope or importance for the overall mission of the church. These may go on to implementation without going through all of the steps outlined above. But those that have far-reaching consequences usually go through each of these steps, and may take a year or more before moving toward implementation. This is why it is important that a pastor is thinking several years ahead, and not merely toward the upcoming year. Ideally the implementation of the vision occurs simultaneously with the need or opportunity beginning to present itself to the casual observer. This may be several years after the pastor first initiated discussion about the vision.

Remember, as you are moving through this process, the lessons from chapter 12 on dealing with opposition and conflict. Few leaders move through the visioning process without generating some opposition. Do not be discouraged by this. Listen and learn from those who oppose the vision. But if you have strong support for the vision from a large number of your leaders, charge ahead.

8. The Preliminary Plan

It is one thing to have wonderful visions. It is quite another to actually see them materialize into ministry. Sometimes you may hand off a vision to one or more staff members or a lay ministry team and turn them loose on it. Generally, however, it is the job of the leader to outline a preliminary strategy aimed at achieving the vision. This plan need not be detailed, but it should demonstrate your knowledge of the broad steps, the struggles, and the issues that will need to be addressed, along with a reasonable time frame for fulfilling the plan. When our church was smaller, I nursed many of the plans from visioning to implementation, working with a team of laypeople, or, in some cases, leading the charge myself. Today more than half of the visions and goals I set each year are handed off to other groups to implement. Both the preliminary and final plans should be brought before the church's leadership council for review and approval if the vision is a major effort.

9. Enlisting the Cavalry

Once the vision is fully formed, and before it is taken to the general congregation, it is important to find key laypeople who will help lead the charge to see the vision fulfilled. Which of the leaders you consulted was most excited about the vision? This person is an obvious choice to help. You will also want to scan your congregation for persons who have special skills in the areas you need. Finally, having influential lay leaders that others in the congregation know and trust is important. Recruiting these persons, helping them know your reasons for choosing them, and emphasizing the importance you place on the vision and on their leadership will help ensure success. Help this group to truly grasp the vision, but at the same time use them to perfect it and help develop the strategy to see the vision become reality.

10. Selling the Vision

By the time you get to this stage, in a small church, a large number of your members will already be aware of the vision. But they may not be completely informed about the rationale, the plan, or the end result. It is easy for members who have only some of the facts to begin shooting down the vision for lack of adequate information. They typically raise questions that you have already considered many times through the discernment process. This points to the need for excellent communication, accompanied by the opportunity for persons to ask questions. It is important that both the pastors and the key leaders or support team not become defensive in the face of these questions. Viewing this period of questioning as a positive is very important, though not always easy to do when members attempt to shoot down the plan.

Your case for pursuing the vision should always begin with the mission of the church and a clear mandate from the Scriptures. After all, you are claiming that this is your understanding of God's vision for your church. It should include a positive affirmation of your congregation and its gifts, since this vision was developed in part because of the potential you saw in its members. Your presentation to the congregation should include a clear presentation of the need or opportunity; paint a picture of how the world will be different as a result of pursuing the vision. In the process remind the congregation that the most meaningful and greatest ministry opportunities almost always require sacrifice, change, and a willingness to risk failing.

Obviously the complete process just described is used primarily for introducing major initiatives and visions. Many visions you have as a leader will be readily embraced and will require only a few of these steps. My challenge to you, the reader, is to dream "God-sized" dreams. Too many churches dream small, safe, easily attainable dreams. They don't risk, they don't require faith, they don't need God in order to be accomplished. The church I serve has experienced significant ministry in its first ten years. Nearly all of the most important initiatives and key decisions were a result of the process outlined above.

All of the most critical decisions were those that were a bit frightening, often leaving me with a knot in my stomach, and knowing there was no way we could accomplish the vision without God's help. Steve Camp, a contemporary Christian artist has called this, "living dangerously in the hands of God." I've been there many times. And God has always taken me beyond what I had dared to imagine or believe!

FOURTEEN

What You Need to Know About Staff

Most pastors receive little formal training in managing staff. I can recall only one class period in my entire seminary training devoted to ministry in a multiple-staff setting. While I was in seminary, managing staff was the farthest thing from my mind. I anticipated that my first church would be a small, rural church and I would be lucky if I had a part-time secretary. When I started Church of the Resurrection in 1990 I was two years out of seminary and I had neither managed another human being in my life nor had I attended an entire meeting of the staff-parish relations committee. Today we have 140 staff members and a human resources department! In this chapter I'd like to offer a few pointers for pastors, church staff members responsible for managing other staff, and lay committees responsible for staffing in the local church. Your ministry setting will be very different from mine, but I believe some of the insights shared in this chapter will be of value to almost any church.

The Pastor and the Personnel Committee

It must be clear to the staff and to the personnel committee that the senior pastor is the leader of the staff. Any other arrangement will ultimately fail because it will produce staff who are loyal to a personnel committee but who feel they can bypass the senior pastor. While a grievance policy might ultimately allow the staff to go to a personnel committee, this is a measure of last resort. Grievances should never get to that point, for once they have, the relationship between the senior pastor and the staff member is likely already beyond repair. Either the senior pastor or other staff with supervisory responsibilities, or both, are responsible for managing the staff, for setting goals and priorities, for conducting evaluations and reviews, and for making compensation recommendations. The personnel committee will play an important part in this process as the senior pastor works with it. But it is important that the committee not try to manage the staff directly. The role of the personnel committee in the church is to set policies, to assist in recruiting, to interview and hire the best staff possible for the church, to create an outstanding work environment in which staff can thrive, to set compensation for staff in conjunction with the senior pastor's input and recommendations, and to provide guidance, feedback, and support for the senior pastor and, through him or her, for the staff.

Our staff-parish relations committee has played a critical role in the growth and development of our church. The visionary leadership of the committee members, and their willingness to work with me in fulfilling the visions and dreams God has given us, have been extraordinary. Their philosophy has always been, "How can we do more for our staff? What can we do to bless and encourage them? What would it take to hire and keep the best staff possible? How can we help and support your ministry, Adam?" This approach to staffing is one of the keys to the success of our congregation. The senior pastor helps to shape this committee and its perspectives. In The United Methodist Church the senior pastor is the chair of the nominating committee. As such the staff-parish relations committee is one of several groups that I have placed a special emphasis upon. I look for people with management and personnel experience who have completely bought into the vision of the church and who are visionary people themselves. I look for those who are deeply committed to Christ. I steer clear of people who have an agenda, an ax to grind, or who have a history of confrontation with multiple staff members.

The Senior Pastor's Role in Leading the Staff

The senior pastor plays a critical role for the rest of the staff. You set the tenor for the staff. The staff must respect you and your leadership. They must believe that you are truly seeking to follow Christ and that you genuinely love them.

Your task, as it relates to staff, is to constantly remind them of the goal that your church is working toward (your mission or purpose), to help them see their role in accomplishing that goal, and to inspire confidence in them that together with God's help, you can achieve those goals. Your staff must feel that you are in their corner. They must know you are proud of them, and they must believe that you want the best for them and for the church.

Your task will also include recruiting great staff. I personally recruited nearly all of our early staff. I was constantly looking for people who were demonstrating leadership through their volunteer work in the church. I looked for people whose passion was doing God's work. Some had never considered working on a church staff before and I had to plant the seeds of the idea, then water those seeds, and finally help the individuals see the difference they would make for Christ's kingdom. Many of our staff left jobs in the corporate world paying twice what we pay. Why would some people take a 50 percent pay cut to come and work for the church? Because they want to change the world and to use their talents to help others meet Christ. Once again, if you, the pastor, and the church are clearly focused and passionate about the church's biblical mission, your church will attract a higher caliber of people who will want to work on your staff and will be willing to sacrifice greatly in order to do so.

In order to recruit and retain great staff, you must offer regular examples of how each person's work is helping to minister to people. Every year at our annual staff Christmas party I read E-mail or tell stories from congregants whose lives have been changed by the church's ministry. (I keep a file for this purpose containing E-mail and notes I receive throughout the year.) I intentionally lift up stories about staff members who may not otherwise hear of the impact of their ministry.

> **My aim is to be relatively hands-off, to empower the staff to make critical decisions for their ministry areas.**

Recently, I shared the story of a woman who spoke of how encouraged she was by our custodian, who always spoke kindly to her and offered to help her whenever she needed it. Our entire custodial staff felt encouraged by this. I spoke of the small child who, every time her family drives past the church notes, "That's my church! That's my church!" This child is in our preschool, and I went on to speak of how many lives had been changed by our preschool ministry. I had one congregant who had told me that she really didn't ever need to speak to a pastor when she had a pastoral care concern because our administrative assistants and secretaries knew just how to minister to her when she called. As I told that story you could see the smiles on the faces of our administrative support team. One by one I told stories about each ministry area, to remind them that the sacrifices they make in ministry are worth it, and that I as their pastor know how important their work is.

In addition to keeping the staff focused on the church's purpose, you are also the spiritual leader and mentor of the staff. Your aim is to see that your staff are growing in Christ. You may even have some staff who don't know Christ yet (this is sometimes true in the custodial and support staff areas).

We have developed several tools that help us offer spiritual nurture to our staff. One of these is our weekly Staff Chapel. One morning each week we invite all of the staff in the building to join us for a time of worship. We usually have anywhere from forty to sixty people in attendance. We begin the service by introducing new staff and welcoming them. We then sing two or three hymns. Next we invite the staff to share their joys and concerns. We pass out the intercessory prayer request cards that were turned in by our congregation members in the prior weekend's worship service—each staff member receiving two or three—and we spend time in silent prayer, lifting up our fellow staff and our congregation members. I close this time in prayer, praying specifically for those staff who lifted up a concern. Then we move to a twenty-minute study of the Scriptures. This year we have gone chapter-by-chapter through the New Testament, and we invite different staff to prepare and lead the study. We close with one last hymn and prayer and then a time when I can share any important news or information or words of encouragement. This is a time for me to keep the staff focused on our purpose while helping them feel that they are "in the know" on what's happening in the church. The entire service lasts about an hour. We end by inviting staff to share signs of peace—to hug a few necks before they go!

Another way we seek to spiritually mentor our staff is through our staff meetings. Every member of the staff is a part of a staff team. Most of these staff meetings are held weekly. I lead the executive staff meeting that is held on Wednesday mornings from 10:00 A.M. until noon, followed, when possible, by lunch. This team includes my executive assistant and the executive directors of each of our major ministry divisions. We begin by sharing joys and concerns, followed by a time of scripture study in which we discuss the daily scripture readings from the study guides handed out in worship (see chapter 7). We do this as a way of holding one another accountable for actually reading the scriptures daily. Next, staff bring to the table items for discussion from their ministry areas. This serves both to keep me informed and give me the opportunity to provide any feedback or direction they need from me. My aim is to be relatively hands-off, to empower them to make critical decisions for their ministry areas. Finally, I will bring up any concerns or ideas that I may have, or visions for new or emerging ministries, and solicit their feedback.

This meeting serves to develop a sense of team among our lead staff, to hold them accountable for pursuing the spiritual disciplines, to facilitate communication between them and their departments, to share ideas, and to foster an environment where effective ministry can take place. Our executive directors then hold staff meetings once a week with their direct reports, aimed at accomplishing these same goals. Their direct reports then hold staff meetings with their ministry teams. Most of our full-time staff will have spent a total of four to five hours in staff meetings throughout the week—one hour in staff chapel, two hours with his or her supervisor and other direct reports, and then another one to two hours with those who report to him or her. Most of our part-time staff and support staff will only attend staff chapel and their own staff meetings with their supervisors, thus spending no more than two hours a week in staff meetings.

This will seem excessive to those in small and mid-sized churches. The larger the church becomes, however, the more critical communication is. We developed this system after a period in which our staff morale and satisfaction had fallen. As we studied this phenomenon we discovered that many staff did not feel that they were a part of a ministry team, they did not feel like they were an important part of the ministry of the church, and they were frustrated by a lack of communication. This current staff structure seems to have addressed these concerns. Though your setting may be much smaller, there are key concepts in what I've just described that will translate into your ministry setting. These include the need your staff will have for accountability, communication, the feeling of being a part of a team, and fellowship. One way or another you will need to plan to meet these needs.

For Very Large Churches ONLY: A Crash Course in Organizational Design

A note to the reader: The following section may only prove helpful for the largest churches. It may be of interest to others, and a challenge to see if you are able to discern translatable principles from this section for your own church.

I've been speaking about Church of the Resurrection's staffing and our "executive directors," but it may be helpful for you to know something of our staff structure and organizational design. Some reading this book will be very familiar with these terms and ideas. For some of you this may be new territory. An organizational design or structure is, at a very simple level, an "org.chart"—it lays out the relationship between the staff of an organization. But underneath this simple definition is something much more complex, for an organizational structure is about how staff are managed and led, how communication takes place within an organization, how conflicts are resolved, and how people work together. These issues are important in any sized church. In small churches the answers to these questions are relatively simple and easy to define. But as your church grows, or you move to a larger church, the church's organizational design or structure will become critical, for the issues of who manages whom, where various responsibilities are laid, and how communication takes place become more complex and require much more intentionality and a structure to ensure that each is adequately dealt with. An effective organizational design can allow for ministry to flow smoothly and efficiently and foster a wonderful work environment. An ineffective organizational design can be disastrous, leading to confusion, conflict, staff burnout and breakdown. In 1999 and early 2000, our church found itself headed toward the latter as a result of an organizational design that the church had outgrown.

Between 1997 and early 2000 our church grew from two thousand in worship per weekend to five thousand in worship per weekend. During this period of time we added seventy full- and part-time staff people. We had always been a very flat organization, meaning that we would add program staff but did not add any managers to support them. At first I was proud that we were a "lean" organization—heavy on ministry personnel and light on management. But there came a time when this no longer served us well. We were undermanaged.

Most large churches, at several times during their growth phase, will reach a point where the organizational design no longer meets the needs of the church. One of the first major organizational overhauls may come when the church begins employing six or seven full-time program staff. These staff will need someone to manage and coordinate them. Ideally this would be the senior pastor, but some pastors have little or no skill in this area, while others will not have the time to fulfill the management functions necessary to support these staff. If this is the case, then the church may need to hire its first manager. In many churches this person will not only function as a business administrator, overseeing operations, but will also handle the coordination and management functions of the lead staff.

Later when the business functions become larger and the staff numbers twelve to fourteen full-time program positions, a church may need a second manager, often called an executive pastor or administrative pastor. This person may come from the corporate world or be a trained ministry professional who has outstanding management skills. Occasionally an existing program staff member will exhibit exceptional management skills and will be promoted to this new position. Our church had been through both of these phases of growth, and had come to the place where we had about sixteen staff reporting to an executive pastor in addition to a business administrator handling the operational side of the church. Coordination, support, and communication began to break down at this point.

I felt the need to hire a consultant to help us analyze where we were experiencing breakdown. I also wanted the consultant to look at where we were going in the future, anticipating that our staff would double in size in the next five years. This consultant would then help us develop an organizational structure that would serve our church well into the future. Our staff-parish relations committee supported the idea and allocated funds for the project (about $15,000 total). After looking into the backgrounds of various possible consultants, we chose a local firm that one of our staff-parish relations committee members had worked closely with. The consultant utilized some of our own members with expertise in human resources to conduct a series of interviews with all of our staff who worked twenty or more hours per week. (The use of our own members in conducting interviews saved us thousands of dollars, but it was critical that these members handle the interviews with the utmost confidentiality.)

In addition to face-to-face interviews, the consultant administered a written questionnaire to all staff working fewer than twenty hours per week. The results of these interviews were compiled into a report letting us know where we were experiencing stress. The findings were interesting. We found our staff rated "best in class" among the clients our consultant had worked with, in terms of knowing and buying into the purpose of our organization. Our staff were again "best in class" in terms of their commitment to this purpose; they genuinely believe in what they are doing.

On the downside we found that many of our staff were near burnout, and many were working considerably more hours than may have been healthy for them. There was general frustration at a lack of communication and support. And some of our staff felt isolated and disconnected. Some of these issues pointed back to me as their pastor. When it came to their work habits, many of our staff had emulated what they had seen in me. I had worked sixty to seventy hours per week for nearly ten years. Some had received E-mail from me at 3:00 A.M., a fact that they noted and remembered. I had set the example and they felt they had to work just as hard as I was working. Though I frequently told staff that this was not my expectation, my actions spoke louder than my words. And of course I had hired people who were driven, as I was, and passionate about the gospel. (The converse is also true: when a senior pastor does not put forth a significant effort, staff take their cues from the pastor and also tend to put forth less than their best efforts.)

The lack of communication and support came, in part, from the tremendous growth we had seen in our church and staff over a very short period of time. While we were growing and adding staff, we did not change our systems for communication and decision making. In some ways I was still seen as being at the hub of everything that happened. Some staff felt they needed to get my approval for ministries before they could launch them. Others felt they needed my support from the pulpit to help their ministry succeed. But with all of the growth my job changed as well. My appointment schedule was constantly booked six weeks to eight weeks out. There were as many as two hundred E-mail messages coming in a week and the only time left to answer them was late at night. I was working on building projects, acquiring additional land, as well as pursuing the ministry goals I had set for myself. I was being asked to speak more and more at events across the country. Staff could not get access to me except at staff chapel. Our lone executive pastor could not keep up with the demand, nor did he feel empowered to make decisions on his own without running them by me. As I look over this list I am grateful that we were able to recognize the signs of trouble and do something about it before our staff imploded.

Once we had identified some of the problems, we invited our staff to help design the new structure, recognizing that if we changed the structure and added managers, this would affect all of them. Through two all-day conferences with our staff, our consultants helped them to identify the key issues that needed to be addressed by a new structure. The staff offered their ideas on how their departments should be organized under this structure. Finally, the staff identified the key characteristics we needed in any new managers who would join us. There was a great deal of fear among our staff generated by this process. They were particularly concerned that we would become "too corporate." They enjoyed the familial atmosphere, the focus on our purpose, and the less structured work environment. They feared a shift in our culture. They also were concerned about who their new managers would be. Some were concerned that this new structure would further isolate them from me (some of our staff had been here when there was only a handful of staff and we spent a great deal of time together). Finally, a few of our staff viewed the hiring of any new managers as a "demotion." They believed that the addition of a new layer of management meant that they were "one rung lower on the ladder" than they had been before. A few spoke openly to their colleagues against the plan they had helped draft at the very outset.

In the midst of the fear and concern some of our staff forgot the difficulties and frustrations they had been experiencing. There was a great need for reassurance, from me and the staff-parish team, that this organizational change was really in the best interest of the church. In the end we placed all of our ministry areas into one of four divisions, roughly corresponding to the four expectations we have of our members (see chart on the following page). Each division is responsible for working together to maximize our efforts at helping members fulfill these expectations. We gave these four new staff members the title "executive director," which roughly corresponds to the title of "executive vice president" in many small or mid-sized corporations. These four persons, along with my executive assistant, share the staff leadership of the church with me. They are each responsible for managing five to seven senior staff members. Each executive director's staff leads major ministry areas in the church.

Church Council
Senior Pastor

Executive
Assistant

Executive Director of Worship, Pastoral Care, and Prayer

1. Director of Music Ministries
2. Director of Worship Ministries
3. Director of Video Ministries
4. Ordained Pastor of Caring Ministries
5. Ordained Pastor of Caring Ministries
6. Ordained Pastor of Caring Ministries
7. Director of Prayer Ministries

Executive Director of Discipleship, Age-Level Ministries

1. Director of Children's Ministries
2. Director of Student Ministries
3. Director of Singles Ministries
4. Director of Adult Discipleship
5. Director of Men's Ministries
6. Director of Women's Ministries

Executive Director of Equipping, Outreach, and Service

1. Director of Lay Ministries
2. Director of Leadership Development
3. Director of Evangelism
4. Director of Missions
5. Director of Assimilation
6. Director of Catalyst Ministries

Executive Director of Finance and Administration

1. Business Administrator
2. Director of Facilities
3. Director of Human Resources
4. Director of Information Technologies
5. Director of Communications

The executive directors are the communication and coordination hub of the church. They are charged with making sure I know what I need to know to lead the church. They are also asked to make sure that their staff know the essential information from other departments and from me. They are responsible for effectively managing and leading their staff, recruiting new staff, setting goals with their staff, helping to resolve conflict, and providing key assistance in problem solving and strategic planning for their staff.

We conducted a nationwide search for persons to fill these positions. In the end one of the positions was filled by an ordained pastor who came to us from out of state. We felt it was important to have at least one ordained pastor, in addition to myself, as a part of this team. She had experience not only as a district superintendent, but also as a senior pastor of her own church. (At the same time we recognized that ordained clergy are seldom actually trained, equipped, experienced, and gifted in management, and hence the best persons to fill these positions may not be clergy, but rather, committed Christians from the corporate world.)

> It is important to remember, as your church grows, that you will need to make changes both in how you lead and in your organizational design.

One of the directors was an existing staff member who was well respected and known for his integrity. He provided continuity with our other staff and brought to the executive group ten years of experience with our church. This proved invaluable in sharing our culture with this team of persons, three of whom were new to our staff. The final two executive directors were deeply committed laypeople in our church. One came from a regional management position with a large insurance company. He was well known and loved by many of our ministry staff and had been a key volunteer and leader in our church already. The last of our executive directors is a woman who came to us after having served as senior vice president of a major national bank for many years. She, too, had extensive experience in lay leadership in our church, had demonstrated a remarkable commitment to Christ, and brought incredible skills from the corporate world to bear on her work at the church. All of these persons were deeply committed Christians, people of the highest integrity, and extremely gifted managers and leaders.

The process we went through may not ever be helpful to you, but the principles behind it are important in nearly any multiple-staff setting. It is important to remember, as your church grows, that you will need to make changes both in how you lead and in your organizational design. These changes always produce anxiety on the part of the other staff. This is normal. When staff contemplate these changes, the fear of the unknown is nearly always greater than the reality. Some of your staff will not be able to grow with the changes. I knew going into our redesign that some of the staff might not be able to fit in the new structure. My aim was that they not make that decision too prematurely, that they give the new structure a chance. Finally, some of the finest church staff members may not come out of the seminary, but out of corporate America. They will be people who are deeply committed to Christ and exhibit a genuine calling, yet who might never leave corporate America to go to seminary, and who may not have a calling to pulpit ministry, but rather to managing or leading ministries. The role of the pastor as spiritual mentor and guide to the staff becomes even more important, however, when persons make the transition from corporate America to the local church.

While we've only been living in our new structure for less than a year, most of our staff have found it to be a blessing; they feel they have the support they need to be more effective and the communication issues are being addressed. Our staff is healthier and has a higher degree of morale than we've had in a long time. And for me personally, this change has been a lifesaver. I feel that the weight of leading this organization is being borne by six people and not just by me.

Hints, Tips, and Great Ideas in Staffing

In the following section I offer insights, hints, tips, and great ideas that might be helpful for you in your ministry. I'll offer them as bulleted points, but I will expand on several of them.

- *Some of your greatest potential staff people are sitting in your pews. Look for them!*

In the early church local congregations didn't hire staff away from other churches, they recruited, trained, and deployed the people whom the Holy Spirit had gifted from within their own congregation.

- *Two part-time specialists, each focusing on his own ministry area will produce more ministry than one full-time person trying to do both ministries.*

(As your church grows larger you may find that this rule eventually begins to break down as it will ultimately require twice as much managerial support to manage two part-time staff as it will to manage one full-time staff member.)

- *An encouraging thank-you note after a job well done is worth more than a $1,000 raise.*

- *Never correct or discipline a staff member in front of others. Never demean a staff member.*

- *Require a written job description with clear reporting relationships, job responsibilities, and expectations before approving new positions.*

- *When running short of space, staff may share offices. But keep an open mind in looking for additional potential offices.*

At Church of the Resurrection we have renovated electrical closets, storage rooms, and foyers to serve as offices. We utilize special "portable offices" in Sunday school classrooms. (These look like armoires that open to hold a computer, two file drawers, a small bookcase, and a desk, but when closed they lock and look like a nice piece of furniture. Check your office supply catalogs.) We even have some staff who use an office in their homes. This allows us to utilize as much of the building for ministry spaces as possible.

- *Each staff member has her own laptop or desktop computer and voice mail box, reducing the need for secretarial staff.*

In addition, most staff share a secretary with others, and many of our administrative assistants and secretaries are part-time; many are stay-at-home moms who work while their children are in school.

- *Great administrative assistants are worth their weight in gold! Use them but don't abuse them!*

My assistant handles all of my scheduling, keeps my calendar, handles nearly all of my phone calls, and returns my voice mail messages. She protects my time and acts on my behalf. Most people who call don't really need to talk with me; they need to speak with someone else on staff. But once they do reach me, they are so excited that it is not uncommon for a five-minute conversation to become a thirty-minute call. When I began to get up to thirty calls a day, and did nothing but sit with the phone glued to my ear, we realized the need to make a change. My assistant may be the second most important staff person at Church of the Resurrection. She is a project manager, a personal manager, a problem solver, and an invaluable resource. She knows my thought processes so well she can almost always anticipate my response to questions, and she knows what I am going to need even before I do. Pastors, consider taking your administrative assistants and secretaries to the next level. Help them to become true partners in ministry with you and entrust projects to them. They will be energized by this, and so will you!

- *A good, well-thought-out personnel policies manual is a must.*

Develop one, give one to each new employee, and stick to it. We spent several years developing a personnel policies manual; it is the finest I have ever seen and has been through multiple revisions. You may order a copy of it, on disk, to adapt to your church by contacting Church of the Resurrection at *www.cor.org*.

- *Publicly recognize your staff and intentionally seek to praise them and build them up.*

- *Ask your personnel committee for a discretionary fund to enable you to purchase small gifts for your staff at birthdays, anniversaries of employment, or after a remarkable performance.*

These small rewards go a long way in helping staff feel appreciated. Examples of this might be a gift certificate for dinner for the employee and his or her spouse, a nice fountain pen, a book or CD, or even a night's stay at a local hotel. Again a $50 gift may be worth more than a $2,000 pay increase if shared in a timely way with appropriate encouragement and appreciation.

- *If you have a staff member who is experiencing financial difficulty, offer help.*

We have bought batteries for cars, assisted with utilities, or helped with school supplies. But be careful not to create a dependency. This could be unhealthy for both parties.

- *Staff "Fun Days"*

Twice a year we try to provide a few hours on an afternoon to reward the staff and allow them to unwind. Our first two events included an afternoon of bowling, in which the staff-parish relations committee hosted and provided two free games of bowling and free soft drinks and appetizers. This wasn't very expensive, maybe $15 per person, but it was a huge morale builder! In addition, twice a year we will bring in breakfast or lunch for the staff as part of a "staff appreciation day." Each summer we have a family picnic in which all of the staff and their families come together for a meal at a local park on a Friday night. We have entertainment of some kind and games for the kids.

- *Staff Shirts*

Each year we purchase embroidered shirts or sweatshirts with the church's logo under which appears the designation "Staff." These are often worn on Fridays around the office. The staff who appreciate these the most are those who are behind the scenes, the ones who our church members might not otherwise recognize. This form of recognition helps them feel a part of the team.

- *Staff Christmas Party*

From the time we had only two staff people until today we have always had staff Christmas parties. We've gone out to eat, or come to my home. Today, all staff and their spouses or guests meet at the church and enjoy a nice, catered meal. We will have musical entertainment from a local high school choir singing Christmas music. Then we go into the sanctuary for communion and worship. It is a very meaningful evening and the only corporate Christmas party most have ever been to where the wine is used for communion! This event serves another important purpose. Some of the spouses of our staff members are not Christians, or if they are, they don't completely understand why their spouses are working at a church. During the worship service, as I noted earlier in this chapter, we highlight the purpose of the church and the important role each staff member plays in fulfilling this purpose. For many, this is the first time they really understand and appreciate what their spouses do at the church.

- *Staff Retreats*

Twice each year we take those staff who are direct reports either to me or to our executive directors—about thirty staff in all—to a United Methodist retreat center for thirty-six hours of time away. Everyone brings her favorite snack foods and soft drinks. We pay the retreat center to provide two lunches and a breakfast, but I prepare chili for supper. We begin with prayer, then a "fellowship walk" in which we walk through the woods as a group, sharing and talking. From there we spend two hours in quiet solitude. Each staff member is given a pocket-size New Testament and some suggested readings to take with him or her. We return for lunch and fellowship. Next we turn to a planned time for staff enrichment. At our last retreat we had a guide lead us in the Myers-Briggs Type Indicator and, after analyzing the results, he helped us understand the implications of our personality types for our working relationships with one another. We have a bit of free time before supper for reading, napping, or fellowship. After supper we take a hayride, then have worship with Holy Communion. Finally, we have free time for singing, fellowship, or playing cards. The next morning we take an early walk, have devotions, and then focus the day on planning, goal setting, and calendaring. The result of these retreats are huge including spiritual renewal, professional growth, planning, and team building.

- *Conduct Annual Reviews with Your Staff*

Several weeks prior to an employee's annual review we provide her with a "self-evaluation" form, to be filled out and returned a week before the review. This allows the staff member to evaluate last year's goals, and to give an appraisal of her own performance. Usually staff are harder on themselves than you would be on them and the self-evaluation allows them to raise problem areas and gives you the opportunity to respond to them. In preparation for each review the pastor or supervisor spends time in prayer, then looks over the self-evaluation along with the prior year's evaluation. We do not expect staff to complete all of their goals, but we do look for a significant number to be completed each year. Before meeting with the staff member we will add any goals we have for them for the coming year to the list they have generated in the self-evaluation. Finally, we write a letter to the staff member offering encouraging words, and, when necessary, suggesting areas for growth. This process takes between five and ten hours per review in order to do it right. By making good use of this tool you will increase staff productivity and satisfaction with their jobs. Once per quarter meet with your staff to see what progress is being made on achieving their goals.

- *Staff Childcare*

Recognizing that our salaries may be lower than the corporate world, we look for benefits we can offer that help offset this without adding significant costs to the budget. One of these benefits is offering staff childcare. We ask those staff who will make use of childcare to contribute toward the cost at a reduced rate, with the church paying the remaining amount. These employees are thrilled to have their children on-site and are grateful to pay a reduced rate. The program costs the church very little but the dividends are huge.

- *Continuing Education*

We encourage staff to take continuing education seriously. Each part-time program staff member has a $500 allowance per year. Each full-time program staff member has a $1,000 continuing education allowance per year. Both of these amounts need to be increased in the future. The church has provided me with a $3,000 continuing education allowance each year for the last seven years, which can be used for books, subscriptions to journals, and continuing education events. My aim is to attend two such events each year. Some of the events I create myself. I have often made appointments to spend the day with pastors and staff members of churches larger than ours to learn from them. Seldom have I used all of these funds, but I am grateful that the church makes them available.

- *Turkeys at Thanksgiving*

Several years ago we began giving gift certificates for free turkeys at the local grocer to all of our staff. We get a reduced price for buying so many. Again the cost to the church is relatively small, but it is a meaningful gesture for our staff.

- *Sabbatical Leave*

Once every seven years a full-time program staff member qualifies for a sabbatical leave. This leave must be requested in writing the year before, along with a plan for how the time will be used and the goals of the sabbatical. Our sabbatical leave is actually something of an extended study leave. It is anticipated that this time will be used for writing and for extended research in an area that will strengthen the staff member's ministry. The sabbatical leave can last up to three months but must be taken during the summer.

- *Hire the Right Staff Person*

Great staff persons will pay for themselves many times over. Don't try to see how little you can get people to work for; see what is reasonable and pay this. If increasing your compensation by another $5,000 will allow you to attract someone who will double your program, this is money well spent.

- *Employee Orientation*

Often we expect our new employees to hit the ground running in the church. What we found at Church of the Resurrection is that a little more time invested in the orientation process would lead to less frustration and greater productivity. We have a staff member, our director of human resources, who conducts the new-employee orientation with the staff member as he comes on board. At this time, he is given his keys, an overview of the personnel policies (and his own copy), an overview of the benefits offered by the church, a tour of the building, and a chance to talk with someone about his questions.

This is just a bit of what we strive to do to make Church of the Resurrection a rewarding place to work and to help our staff feel appreciated and encouraged. We hope to invest in our people, knowing that our staff is our most valuable resource. I love our staff. I am so proud of them and I believe they truly are the finest church staff in the United States (apart from yours, of course). I have a team of people, most of whom don't have decades of ministry experience. What they have are gifts, passion, heart, and vision. And I thank God every day that I have the opportunity to work with them!

FIFTEEN

Fund-raising

No church will ever reach its full potential unless the pastor is an effective fund-raiser. Unfortunately most pastors are given little or no direction in seminary on fund-raising. The local church pastor is the "chief development officer" for a small to mid-sized nonprofit organization, and yet he or she has no training whatsoever in how to do this! What I will share in this chapter is what I have learned to date having watched our church grow from $40,000 in offerings in our first full year of ministry in 1990 to over $8 million in total offerings in 2001.

The Importance of the Annual Campaign

I have friends who tell me that it has been years since the church they are a part of has conducted a stewardship campaign. They tell me that they don't need a stewardship campaign because the church offerings cover the expenses with a bit of money left over at year's end. Here are my challenges to these church leaders: If you don't need to conduct an annual stewardship campaign in order to accomplish the ministry you've laid out, you are likely not doing all that you could for the kingdom of God. In addition you are not taking seriously your role in discipling people if, in the most materialistic society in the world, you are not addressing the biblical concepts of stewardship each year. And finally, I cannot imagine a church where, if the offerings increased by 15 to 20 percent (a likely outcome for a church that has not conducted a steward-ship campaign for several years), the church could not find *something* creative to do with the money in service to Christ.

If you are not conducting an annual stewardship campaign, you are already underperforming in most areas of your ministry.

The truth is, if you are not conducting an annual steward-ship campaign, you are already underperforming in most areas of your ministry, unless you are confident that all of your church members are already biblical tithers, giving 10 percent of their income to Christ's work each year. If it has been years since you have conducted an annual campaign, your congregation's offerings may be from 20 to 50 percent below where they should be. Annual stewardship campaigns teach discipleship in the area of finances by focusing on biblical stewardship (both tithing but also the role that God intends for money and possessions to play in our lives). The benefit of this campaign for the congregation is increased offerings available for ministry. Before examining the outline of an actual stewardship campaign, I'll begin by taking a look at the issues of pledge cards and confidentiality.

To Pledge or Not to Pledge

At Church of the Resurrection we ask our members to fill out a "commitment card" each fall indicating their anticipated giving for the coming year. Many people are averse to returning a pledge or commitment card, especially if they have not been asked to do this before. We have found that if we explain the reasons for the card, and address their concerns about confidentiality, most people are receptive to filling out the card. In addition, as we share our membership expectations with persons before they join, we always share with them that returning a commitment card is an expectation, and explain the reasons for it, so all of our new members who join the church understand that this will be expected of them. It may take several years for your congregation to completely accept the idea of the commitment card, but if it is presented every year, and if each year the reasoning is explained, a large part of your congregation will return their commitment cards.

Commitment cards (we do not call them pledge cards as we've found people are more responsive to the idea of a commitment rather than a pledge) are very important. In order to fill out a commitment card a member must actually give consideration to his giving in relation to his actual income. The annual stewardship campaign leads every member to spend time praying about her giving, while offering an opportunity to take a step closer to tithing if she is not currently a tither. Having a commitment card requires action in this regard, whereas a campaign without a card might leave persons intending to pray about their commitments without ever getting around to setting an amount or taking a step forward. Filling out and returning commitment cards also serves as a way of expressing a commitment to God; returning the commitment card becomes an act of faith and worship. In addition, returning commitment cards gives the church an opportunity to reliably estimate the next year's income.

In those churches that do not invite people to return commitment cards the church is "guesstimating" what members will give in the next year, based on the prior year's giving. They must make an informed guess as to how much, if any, members will increase their giving. If they have failed to estimate accurately, then the church sends out letters to its members with grim financial reports stating that members need to increase their giving. Churches that ask members to return commitment cards have a reliable number upon which to develop their budgets for the year, not based upon guesses and estimates, but upon the actual indications of the church members. This minimizes the number of times churches must sound the alarm regarding the state of church finances. (One important note: After monitoring our commitments versus actual receipts, we have learned that we must reduce the total commitments by 10 percent each year to account for persons who move or lose their jobs or who otherwise are unable to fulfill their entire commitment.) One final benefit of the commitment card is that people who actually fill out a commitment card are more likely to give more and give it more regularly than those who do not return a card.

Who Has Access to Pledge Information?

While I have access to pledge information as the senior pastor—and I think most of our members assume   this is the case—we do not explicitly state this. The truth is that the pastor seldom needs this information. I cannot think of the last time I have seen a report of either our members' financial commitments or actual giving or both. I could not tell you anyone's pledge in our church today. I can barely remember my own pledge! Nevertheless, there are times when a pastor may need access to this information.

Some church members are concerned with the idea that the pastor would have access to this information. Some church treasurers guard this information and believe it is their job to keep it from pastors. The concern is that this information will potentially taint the pastor's view of certain parishioners, by perhaps being disappointed in their relatively low giving. Typically, the concern lies with the parishioner who may be embarrassed about her low giving. Many church members fear that the pastor will give special attention and cater to those who are the church's largest contributors. The pastor must be aware of this and be cautious about this. The scriptures are clear about the importance of not showing favoritism to the wealthy (see James 2:1-7). (Though often it is not the very wealthy who are the biggest donors to the church.)

There are three times when it is critical for the pastor to have access to information regarding church members' giving. The first is when the church is conducting capital funds campaigns. In these campaigns it is common to approach the church's strongest donors to make leadership gifts in the campaign. In addition the persons who are currently the strongest givers are likely to be the persons who will give the largest gifts to the capital campaign. The second place it is important to have access to giving information is in determining the makeup of the church's stewardship committee. If possible a stewardship committee should include persons who are tithers. If the committee is made up of nontithers, they will always be hesitant to give a strong emphasis to tithing because they themselves are not pursuing this. Finally, if you have individual donors whose contributions make up more than 5 percent of the total church budget it is important that you are aware of this so that in the event that they die or their families move, you can be prepared for the consequences to the church budget.

It is absolutely essential that the commitments and actual giving of your congregation be kept confidential. Only the church's financial secretary, business administrator, and the senior pastor should have access to this information. If these persons are found to share that information with others they should be relieved of their positions. A lack of confidence in the confidentiality of commitments can undermine the church's entire stewardship effort.

An Outline of an Annual Stewardship Campaign

The effective stewardship campaign has several goals. The first is to help members grow in their faith and their commitment to Christ. The second is to teach biblical stewardship. The third is to have each member increase his giving, if possible, so that the ministry of the church may be extended. And the fourth is to have each member return a commitment card. Our stewardship campaigns nearly always occur in late October and November, since, by this point in the year, members will likely have an idea what their next year's income will be. We keep the above goals in mind as we design the campaign. In order to conduct a quality annual stewardship campaign, a budget of $7 to $10 per member household is probably a minimum. This expenditure will be recouped five to ten times over in additional funds given because the campaign was done well. A team of creative people, including the senior pastor, focuses on a theme for the campaign, generally choosing this theme in the spring of the year. The theme must capture the heart and passion of the people. We have often used hymns as the theme, or found hymns that go along with the theme. Some of our campaign themes have included, "Lift High the Cross," "Shine Bright the Light," "Come Dream with Us!" and "Be Thou My Vision." From this meeting we lay out a project schedule for the campaign, working our way backward from commitment weekend. Here's a typical schedule:

Last Monday in October

Letter sent to the congregation from the senior pastor announcing the campaign theme, the reason for the campaign, the goals of the campaign, and the timeline for the effort.

First Sunday in November:
Thank You and Celebration of Ministry Weekend

Campaign theme song introduced. Materials are handed out in worship highlighting the accomplishments of the church in the last twelve months—demonstrating the relationship between giving and ministry. We try to share stories, either through video or testimonial, of how lives have been changed by the church. This weekend we express appreciation for our congregation's faithfulness and invite members to begin praying about their giving for the coming year.

First Monday in November

Mail materials that were handed out in worship to all households. (This is "over-communicating" designed to increase the number of persons who actually read the material. This also allows those members who were not present in worship to see these materials.) Again, the tone of this piece should be one of encouragement, celebration, and thanksgiving. A letter should accompany the piece expressing appreciation for each member's gifts. (We do not send any stewardship materials to non-members, though by handing them out in worship our visitors do receive them and many pledge.)

Second Sunday in November:
Dreams and Visions Weekend

On this weekend we hand out a brochure highlighting our dreams and visions for ministry in the coming year. These have been solicited from the various ministry areas in the church, inviting all leaders to begin dreaming about what they could be doing in ministry in the coming year if the resources were available. We share the most compelling of these with our congregation, both in the brochure, but also in a moving four to six minute video showing clips of ministry taking place around the church. Remember, people give to ministry and mission and to God, not to budgets and salaries and denominational programs. Again we ask our members to pray about and give consideration to the amount of their commitment for the coming year. This weekend I preach a sermon about the role of money in the life of a Christian, focusing on money as a means of accomplishing God's ends in our lives.

Second Monday in November

Mail the dreams and visions materials along with a letter highlighting the reason why these ministries are important and what it would take for the church to accomplish these visions. While we always focus on moving people to tithing, we have also found it helpful to let people know the additional average amount per member household that would be required in order to accomplish these goals (i.e., if the average household increased its giving by just $15 per week, all of these could be accomplished).

Third Sunday in November:
Biblical Stewardship Weekend

On this weekend we will teach about biblical stewardship—what the Bible says about tithing. The key scriptures that I have found helpful include 1 Chronicles 29:14b, 16; Genesis 14:18-20; 28:20-22; Malachi 3:6-12; and especially Leviticus 27:30-32. In the New Testament there are numerous references to giving but little related specifically to tithing. But here are a few of the great New Testament passages: 2 Corinthians 8:1-15; 9:6-15; Luke 12:13-34; 21:1-4; Matthew 25:14-30; Mark 10:17-31; and 1 Timothy 6. We will hand out this weekend what we call our "Guide to Giving," which includes the scriptures above, frequently asked questions about giving, suggestions for how to step forward in giving, and a very tentative budget for the coming year, including our ministry leaders' dreams and visions. We do not list the budget line by line but create a pie chart and place various ministries together, which leaves less room for members to be discouraged from giving because they don't agree with a particular line item. (We do make available our entire budget for those who request it once it is approved.) On this weekend I preach about the tithe and we also have tithers share their testimonies of how they came to tithe. We use videotaped testimonials, which allows us to have some editorial control and enables us to add music and cover video shot at the individual's home or place of employment. Again the service ends with a request that members pray about taking a step forward toward tithing.

Third Monday in November

Mail the frequently asked questions along with the commitment card. A letter should be included explaining once again the reason members are being asked to return a commitment card and expressing the hope that they will increase their giving if possible, moving toward the biblical tithe. The letter should ask members to fill out the card and return it to church the coming weekend.

Fourth Sunday in November: Commitment Weekend

On this weekend our emphasis is on Thanksgiving. We focus on the biblical teachings regarding giving thanks and the sermon is a Thanksgiving sermon. We include a video focusing on gratitude and our giving as an expression of gratitude. The service ends with members returning their commitment cards. A commitment card is included in each bulletin (again, we are overcommunicating, assuming that some members will forget to bring their cards to worship). For all who return their cards this weekend we give a coffee mug as an expression of gratitude for their faithfulness in giving. We also include a small sticker that they can place on their shirts or coats, akin to the "I voted" or "I gave blood" concept. Our stickers include the logo and theme for the stewardship campaign.

Fourth Wednesday in November: Follow-up Begins

We mail a follow-up letter, a commitment card, and a self-addressed stamped envelope to all member households that did not return a commitment card indicating that we had not yet heard from them, and expressing our hope that they will mail the card in during the next week. We found that by placing a stamp on each envelope we may waste some postage but this cost will be more than offset by the number of people who place the card in the mail because it was already stamped.

That's our annual campaign in a nutshell. We preach two sermons focused specifically on giving—and even these are aimed at discipleship rather than the church budget. We include video testimonials from actual tithers. We present our dreams and hopes for ministry in the coming year. And then we "ask for the sale." Do people complain? Yes, usually we have several families each year who are offended because we are talking about money, or they complain because we "spent too much money on fancy brochures." My experience is that often these are people who complain because they feel guilty about their own stewardship. Do *not* let them dissuade you from doing a good job with stewardship. Know that this is part of the price of leadership (remember chapter 12). One last word about this to pastors and church leaders: Remember, you cannot lead people where you yourself are not going.

> **Remember, you cannot lead people where you yourself are not going. You must become a tither.**

You must become a tither. You must freely be able to tell your story. Tell how it was difficult for you to become a tither, but explain the joy you receive from it now. Tell your congregation that you know firsthand the sacrifice that is involved. Until you are tithing you will never preach tithing like you mean it.

Capital Funds Campaigns

Even after your congregation members have taken a leap forward in their offerings, they are probably capable of giving additional funds if a critical need were to arise. For many churches that critical need is additional facilities. As you consider building additional ministry spaces, it is important that you study the possibility of conducting a capital funds campaign. Most congregations can raise between one and one-half and four times their annual operating receipts across the course of a three-year capital funds pledge campaign. Thus, if your current annual offerings are $100,000, it should be possible to raise $150,000 to $400,000 in pledges, to be given over a three-year period of time, over and above your congregation's regular tithes and offerings, in order to build. Your measure of success will depend both on what you are building and the level of support you have among the congregation for the building project. If you are building a new sanctuary you will likely be on the high side of this number. If you are raising funds to reduce debt, you may reach only one and one-half times your annual operating budget.

Typically people are able to make gifts to a special capital funds drive in one of three ways. First, they may be inspired to give some of their accumulated wealth—such as land, shares of stock, or savings—to the church. (After the huge gains in the stock market in the 1990s, a large number of people across the country were able to make significant gifts of appreciated stock that they never would have dreamed possible in the past.) By giving shares of stock or land directly to the church, the donor avoids paying capital gains taxes while gaining a charitable contribution, which means that the cost of the gift was significantly less to the donor than the amount the church received. Of course donors must speak to their own financial planners regarding this. You as a pastor or church leader must be aware of these things but you cannot give financial advice.

A second way people give is by making a sacrifice in their current lifestyle, so they can give out of their regular income. This might include postponing the purchase of a new car (this is what my wife and I did in our first building effort for the church, enabling us to give the equivalent of a car payment each month for three years as we postponed our new car purchase), or not eating out, or choosing to cut back in other planned or actual expenditures. Finally, a third way persons often give to a capital funds campaign is to generate new forms of income to give to the church. Some persons take on extra part-time work, or work overtime when it is available, in order to give to the church.

I have heard from pastors in rural areas saying that such an approach wouldn't work outside of the city; that small-town folk and farmers wouldn't be willing to consider this. At the same time I know one farmer from a small town in Kansas who recently made a $1 million gift to a nonprofit organization in its capital funds drive! Yes, even farmers are open to giving in this way and many of the people in   your local church are likely at an age and stage in life where they could afford to make substantial gifts, if they felt their gifts would have a significant impact for God's kingdom.

Do We Hire a Professional Fund-raising Consultant?

If your church intends to raise more than $300,000 you should consider hiring a professional fund-raising consultant. Pastors and churches who believe that this is an unnecessary expense are sadly mistaken. Most churches that attempt to raise funds on their own will only raise 40 to 60 percent of the amount they would have raised had they used a professional. The question to ask is not "How much will a consultant cost us?" but "How much will it cost if we don't use a consultant?" If you could have raised $400,000 but only raise $200,000 the cost of not using a consultant was $200,000! We have used consultants in four capital funds campaigns and are now preparing for a fifth. Some of the firms that do capital funds campaigns include Resource Services Inc. (RSI), Cargill Associates, The Genesis Group, Inc., Horizons Stewardship Co., INJOY, and a host of others. Most mainline denominations also have professional fund-raisers available for use by local churches. For churches looking to raise less than $300,000 the use of denominational consultants may be the only viable option. The cost of using a professional firm will vary depending on the size of the congregation. There are actually two costs—the cost for the consultant and the cost for printing, video production, and festivities surrounding the commitment event (usually a banquet of some kind). The total cost of these two expenses should not be more than 10 percent of funds raised. The larger the amount you are seeking to raise, the less the total cost of raising funds. Most of our capital campaigns cost less than 3 percent in total. The consultant's fees will not be set as a percentage of what is raised. Instead the fee will be determined by the number of hours the consultant will spend with the congregation, the travel expenses for the consultant, and other overhead and profit. I consider myself an experienced fund-raiser but I would not consider running a capital campaign without the services of a professional firm.

Planned Giving

The last of the stewardship issues that should be mentioned relates to planned giving. In 2000 a mid-sized church in Georgia received a planned gift of $60 million from a member who left most of his estate to the church in his will! Imagine what your church might have done for the kingdom of God had it had these funds available! All of your current church members will die one day. Most will have an estate that they will pass on to someone. If they have not adequately planned for this event, the greatest recipient of these funds will be the Internal Revenue Service. Many of these persons would be interested in giving a portion of their estates to continue the work of the church after their deaths, but they simply have not considered this possibility. At the very least, committed Christians should consider giving a tithe of their estate at death. But it is likely that the only way your members will consider this is if you and the leaders of the church actually take the initiative to suggest it and to help them do something about it.

Many larger churches now have staff members focused on doing this work and helping with annual stewardship campaigns. Others have teams of laypeople who are a part of a planned giving task force. In the end the pastor will often play a key role in raising this issue to the congregation as a whole and in approaching specific members. Consider recruiting one of your most influential senior adults to make a planned gift, and then lead the effort for the church. This member may want to invite the other senior adults to join her for coffee at her home. At this event she should share what she has done and why. The pastor's role is then to cast a vision of how these funds might be used in the future to continue the work of the church and its ministry. Have a list of attorneys or financial planners available in the event that a member does not already have an attorney or financial planner.

SIXTEEN
The Qualities of an
Effective Pastor

There have been many attempts to outline the qualities of
effective leaders. What is interesting is that whether in business,
politics, or in the church, the lists are virtually identical. I am
continually refining and redefining this list, but here are at least
a few of the qualities that are essential for Christian leadership
in the church.

Integrity

Stephen L. Carter of the Yale Law School, in his book,
Integrity, defines this characteristic as "*discerning* what is right
and what is wrong; . . . *acting* on what you have discerned, even
at personal cost; and . . . *saying openly* that you are acting on your
understanding of right from wrong" ([New York: Basic Books,
1996], p. 7). Bill Hybels captured this idea well in one of his books
when he spoke of the person you are when no one else is
looking. Integrity is making sure that who you say you are and
who you really are are one and the same. I appreciated the
comments of one staff person of a church I visited, in describing
his senior pastor. He said, "The people who know my pastor best
respect him the most." That is integrity. For pastors this means
that you practice what you preach!

Humility

Leaders tend to be aggressive/assertive types ("type A"). But
great leaders temper this with genuine humility. They have to
work at this—and sometimes they struggle with it. But the best
genuinely see themselves as servants for others, and strive to
put the needs of others before their own. They strive to avoid
arrogance and egotism. They are cautious in taking too seriously
the positive strokes they will sometimes receive from others.
They don't focus on themselves. Their humility and concern for
others actually cause others to want to follow them, and inspires

loyalty from their coworkers, their employees, or their constituents. This is in strong contrast to some Christian leaders today who act as prima donnas, who seem to have forgotten that we are merely instruments God has chosen to use. I have found that the more "success" I have seen in my ministry the more important it is to continually remind myself that this success is God's doing and not my own. I am aware of the gifts that I possess, but also know that even these gifts came from God. The scriptures teach us this in 1 Peter 5:5b-6, "And all of you must clothe yourselves with humility in your dealings with one another, for 'God opposes the proud, but gives grace to the humble.' Humble yourselves therefore under the mighty hand of God, so that he may exalt you in due time." Both James and Peter quote the passage from Proverbs 3:34, and Jesus clearly emphasized this same point frequently in his ministry.

> Great leaders' humility and concern for others actually cause others to want to follow them, and inspires loyalty from their coworkers, their employees, or their constituents.

Passion

Leaders truly believe in what they are doing; they have convictions. But leadership goes beyond mere convictions to the ability to inspire others with those convictions. This is as true in the business world as in the church world. People love to follow passionate leaders. Great leaders have passion and can inspire others.

Vision

Leaders see things that others do not see. They see opportunities others miss. They anticipate problems before they become problems. They know how to think strategically. They see potential others simply do not see. Vision requires prayer and discernment, a clear understanding of an organization's purpose, the constant practice of benchmarking and learning from others who are "best in class," an accurate perception of the unrealized potential and opportunities for the church's ministry to its members and to the world, and time to think and dream. Many pastors could be visionaries if only they took the time to do the things necessary in order to dream God-sized dreams.

Perseverance

Leaders never give up on anything critical without a fight. They know that there will always be opposition and roadblocks to accomplishing great things. They don't run over people, but they are also not deterred at the first sign of opposition and they don't allow temporary setbacks and defeats to determine their future. As I noted in chapter 12, every great biblical leader faced opposition; what made them great was their perseverance in the face of it.

Decisiveness and Risk Taking

Leaders make decisions. In church settings pastors must make key decisions on the direction the church should go before ever leading others. Some decisions are easy to make. Most important decisions require research, study, prayer, a clear focus on the aims of the organization, and a willingness to take a risk. Risk taking is a part of leadership. When you make decisions you risk being wrong. When you establish new directions for your church's ministry, you will nearly always be risking failure or worse. Pastors must always weigh the risks and rewards of their decisions, and they must also be willing to fail. The most critical decisions that led to the success of Church of the Resurrection were always fraught with risk. Churches can experience paralysis when a risk-averse, indecisive pastor is at the helm.

Being Purpose-Driven

Rick Warren's book *The Purpose-Driven Church* is the book most effective pastors wish they had written. If you have not read Warren's book, it should be next on your reading list. Sometimes the word *driven* is used in a negative sense (see Gordon MacDonald's *Ordering Your Private World*—another excellent book—for the negative sense of drivenness), but here I mean those leaders whose hearts beat and whose deepest desires are to see the church faithfully pursuing God's purposes. This focus on God's purpose for the church energizes them and gives them a clarity that is critical in decision making and leadership. Purpose-driven leaders align resources including staffing, facilities, and finances, as well as their own time, to accomplish the purpose or mission of their organizations as they understand them.

Communication Skills

Effective church leaders, especially pastors, are nearly always effective communicators. This is essential in the pulpit, but is also critical in nearly every other aspect of church leadership. Effective pastors and church leaders have strong interpersonal skills, sometimes demonstrated by initiating conversations with parishioners rather than waiting for others to speak first. They make good eye contact. They demonstrate strong listening skills

> I have known pastors who, after years of ministry, were spiritually empty— and I have, at times, been one of them.

so that others feel heard by them. Effective church leaders are often excellent salespeople; they can communicate their visions in a way that inspires and motivates others to work together to realize these dreams.

Encouragement and Mentoring

People love to be encouraged. Great leaders know how to encourage others. They constantly praise others and build them up. They love to help others succeed and be their best. They exercise restraint in criticism but pursue praise and encouragement with a passion. Part of this quality and mission of encouraging others is used to mentor and develop other strong leaders around you. Successful leaders mentor others and help others hear God's call into ministry. In addition, successful leaders are not threatened by other strong and talented leaders, but instead seek to surround themselves with high-caliber people.

A Personal Relationship with Jesus Christ

It would be very difficult to lead a congregation of Christians to "grow in the grace and knowledge of our Lord Jesus Christ," if the pastor is not doing this herself. This is the most important characteristic of effective pastors and church leaders; it is the foundation upon which the rest of the ministry will be built. Unfortunately, maintaining and growing in your faith while giving yourself in Christian ministry is harder than most people imagine. Sometimes our lives become so busy doing good things for God that once we are finished with our "work" we don't have the desire to then devote the personal time to pray, meditate on the Scriptures, listen for God's voice, or worship the Lord. Like exercise, the longer we go between our quiet times in prayer and scripture study, the more we dread starting our quiet times again. I have known pastors who, after years of ministry, were spiritually empty—and I have, at times, been one of them. When this happens, we lose the joy in our work, we become resentful, tired, frustrated, and ineffective. Effective church leaders pursue the spiritual disciplines, are involved with others in accountability groups, and earnestly seek to grow in their relationship with Christ.

There are many characteristics of effective leaders that I have failed to mention in this list. Perhaps you can come up with your own list. But seldom will effective pastors and church leaders be found who do not possess and exercise a large number of these qualities.

SEVENTEEN

Avoiding Burnout and Other Personal Advice

When I was in seminary one of my professors gave a presentation on clergy burnout. I don't remember the presenter, but one part of the presentation has always stuck with me. The presenter spoke of a study that was done in the mid-1980s on young pastors on the "fast track"; that is, senior pastors who were serving churches with several thousand members very early in their ministries. What I recall was that of the several dozen pastors studied, only one had not succumbed to burnout or moral failure: Walker Railey.

You may recall Walker's story—the powerful and charismatic pastor of First United Methodist Church of Dallas who, during my final year of seminary at Southern Methodist University in Dallas, was receiving death threats. He wore a bulletproof vest and Dallas police officers were present when he preached his Easter sermon that year. I was quite proud of this pastor who was standing in harm's way because of his stand on civil rights. And he was so young to have been appointed to such a large and influential pulpit. Not long after that Easter Sunday Walker's wife Peggy was found nearly strangled to death, and continues to live in a persistent vegetative state to this day. Within days Walker attempted suicide and left a note speaking of the "demons" that had plagued him. As the investigation into Peggy's brutal attack continued, Walker became the prime suspect. It was reported that he had been having an affair with a psychologist. Eventually Railey was found not guilty in the criminal case, but was found liable in a separate civil case. He lost his children, his wife, and his ministry. I keep a file on Walker in my office—a reminder of what can happen when things go wrong in a successful young pastor's life.

There are, of course, hundreds of stories of pastors who have lost their way. Some were "successful" pastors of large churches. Some were bishops and denominational leaders. Some were ordinary pastors serving small and mid-sized churches. Some succumb to moral failure; some to burnout. While these are the exception, not the rule, every pastor who has been in the ministry for any length of time will have been plagued by these same demons and will have flirted with disaster on many occasions. Most have said, "There but for the grace of God go I."

During the first ten years of ministry at Church of the Resurrection I worked long hours, running at a fast pace. I kept telling myself, "Slow down. Be a marathon runner, not a sprinter." But it was hard to slow down. There were always more people to see, more ministries to start. Even after we added staff this only freed me up to do more ministry and pursue other visions for the church. The truth is that we would not be where we are today as a church were it not for the sixteen-hour days and the seventy-hour weeks of those early years. Like an entrepreneur starting a new business, successful new ventures require extraordinary efforts. Success did come. Within a year of its founding the church became the fastest growing United Methodist church in our area. Four years later it became the fastest growing United Methodist church in the country. By the age of thirty I was pastoring the largest church, by worship attendance, in the conference. Accolades followed—the Denman Award, the Circuit Rider Award, the Distinguished Evangelist Award from The United Methodist Foundation for Evangelism. When the newspapers and local media needed a quote from a pastor, they called me. By the age of thirty-five I was pastoring the second largest United Methodist church, by worship attendance, in the United States. Invitations to speak were coming in constantly. I had publishing offers from two publishers. It was all very heady stuff. But in the back of my mind I remembered Walker Railey, and something that Jesus said, "What good will it be for a [person] if [he or she] gains the whole world, yet forfeits [the]

> **Every pastor who has been in the ministry for any length of time will have been plagued by these same demons and will have flirted with disaster on many occasions.**

soul?" (Matthew 16:26 NIV). I would like to offer the following bits of advice to pastors, church leaders, and seminary students regarding the issues of avoiding burnout, caring for yourself and your family, and how not to "gain the world and lose your soul." I offer these as bullet points with a bit of commentary on each.

On Staying Grounded

- *Surrender your life to Christ daily.*

I use a modified version of John Wesley's Covenant Prayer as I walk to work each morning, "Lord, I give my life to you again today. Do with me whatever you will. I pray that you will use me to minister to your people. Help me to bring honor to your name. And grant me a humble heart." This has become something of a ritual for me each morning, but I think that God has honored this prayer and desire of my heart.

- *Don't let success go to your head.*

Remember that you are only a tool—God is the one who is at work in and through you. God could just as easily have used someone else.

- *Minimize the use of your name and your photo in church materials and publicity.*

I always admired this about Billy Graham, the fact that he requested that his photograph appear no more than two or three times in any of his magazines or publications. The more your photo and name appear in the church's advertisements and publications the more the church is about you, and the easier it is for you to become caught up in this.

- *Never set numerical goals for your church or ministry.*

Numbers are the *product* of quality ministry, not the goal. Setting numerical goals is a function of pride or a desire for achievement. In the planning process at Church of the Resurrection we study to see what the likely outcome is, numerically. This is important for planning purposes. But our aim is never going to be about reaching a certain number. Our focus will be on quality ministry.

- *Avoid setting comparative goals.*

When you say that you want to be "the best" or have "the most" or be "the biggest" you are saying that you want your ministry to be better than someone else's. This may be an adequate goal in the corporate world, but in the church world your goal cannot be to be "number one," it must be to do ministry as well as you can in fulfilling your mission. You can strive to be *your best* but not to be *the best.* It is true that you may very well long to learn from others and to do things as well as anyone else, but not for the sake of competing with them, but for the sake of doing kingdom work as effectively as possible. This may seem only a matter of semantics to some, but it is a matter of the heart to me. I have a very competitive nature. I love to play to win. It would be so natural for me to want my church to be bigger and better than anyone else's. I have spent the last ten years trying to submit this competitiveness and ambition to God. God has yet to take this side of me away, but he has used it for his purposes. At the same time the one restraint to this competitive spirit is to reinforce, with words, that we are not competing with others, only aiming to be the best we can be.

- *Take an interest in others, seeking to encourage them and build them up.*

When in conversation with others listen more than you speak, and invite them to tell you of their successes. Speak sparingly about your own. This requires real discipline for some of us who crave affirmation and recognition, but it is a discipline that gets at the heart of humility. Among my favorite scriptures to study in this vein are Paul's writings, especially Philippians 2:3-4, "Do nothing out of selfish ambition or vain conceit, but in humility consider others better than yourselves. Each of you should look not only to your own interests, but also to the interests of others" (NIV). Paul then quotes the beautiful Christ hymn. Sometimes the virtues we want to *feel* in our heart—love, kindness, compassion, forgiveness—are only formed when we first *practice* them on others. God has ways of humbling those who become proud. My aim is to be aware of my pride and ambition, to yield it to God, and to do what I can to cultivate a heart of true humility. Am I there yet? No. I've found true humility to be quite elusive. And so I keep practicing the suggestions I've just offered you.

On Avoiding Burnout, Spiritual Bankruptcy, and Moral Failure

I have heard the story of two bishops sitting in a congregation listening to a young "rising star" preacher. Everyone was most impressed with this young man. The one bishop said to the other, "That's quite a preacher you've got there!" To which the first bishop replied, "Yes, but unfortunately he's got far more in the showroom than he's got in the stockroom." Perhaps the same could be said of most of us at some time or another in our spiritual journey. Every time that I have experienced burnout or spiritual emptiness and the side effects that go with this (writer's block, irritability, frustration, depression, despondency, and discouragement, as well as a host of others), it has come when one of the following has taken place in my life:

1. I am physically exhausted, having gone too many nights with too few hours sleep and having put in too many hours on the job.
2. I have been away from my family doing church work consistently over a period of time.
3. I have not spent quality time in prayer and meditation.

Unfortunately it is when one or more of these conditions have been met that I am at my weakest when it comes to resisting temptation. So, here's a bit of what seems to help get me back on track or keep me from becoming derailed.

- *Spend quality and extended periods of time in prayer.*

I am a poor example of this. I pray as many as ten times in a day, but most of my prayers are the sixty-second variety. But when I begin to "hit the wall" I am reminded of my need to be renewed and strengthened—something that comes, for me, through spending an extended period of time in prayer. For some reading this book this is a common experience; you may do it daily. For some, you may have never done this before. I pursue this prayer time in one of two ways. The first is simply to take a long walk and devote the entire time to conversing with God. I prefer to do this late at night, when no one else is out. For some this may be better done in the morning. I begin with praise and thanksgiving, interspersing prayer and hymns. Sometimes I will set my prayers to the tune of familiar hymns. I then move to sharing from my heart what I am feeling and what I have been experiencing in ministry. In the midst of this I pause, intermittently, to listen for God to speak to me. This happens in the form of thoughts that come into my mind that seem to be in response to my prayer. Finally I lift up concerns for my family, parishioners, and then for myself. This prayer walk is usually about an hour long. While I embark on this walk feeling empty, I always come back feeling renewed. Some would say that this is due to the release of endorphins as a result of the exercise. I have no doubt the physical act of walking does help. But there is something much deeper that occurs that doesn't take place when I simply go for a walk with my wife. I am reminded, after these walks, of the scripture verse, "Those who wait for the Lord shall renew their strength" (Isaiah 40:31). I always come home with my spiritual strength renewed.

> **Perhaps three times a year I will plan a twenty-four- to thirty-six-hour day away in solitude for reading, prayer, and reflection.**

The second way that I pursue an extended conversation with God is on a personal retreat. From time to time my wife will say to me, "You are in need of a prayer retreat." She is able to tell, sometimes even before I am, when my spiritual well is running dry. I am grateful that she encourages me to take this time away. Perhaps three times a year I will plan a twenty-four- to thirty-six-hour day away in solitude for reading, prayer, and reflection. I may go to a church camp nearby, or to a parishioner's farm in the country. I will take bedding, my pocket-size New Testament and my study Bible, a case of soft drinks, a bag of snacks, several notepads, and a couple of books. I may plan to read through a particular book of the Bible while I am away. I begin with an hour-long prayer walk. When I return to the lodge I will read my scriptures and begin writing down the ideas and insights gained. I will go back out for another walk, this time pausing along the way to read through parts of the Bible I've pledged to read. I come back and spend time thinking about the church, our various ministries, upcoming sermons, and I begin writing down more ideas. This will continue—interspersed with reading from the other books I bring and a nap—until late into the evening. The next morning I will pursue this regimen again until the afternoon, when I travel back home. When I come home from these personal retreats I feel reconnected with God and I feel my creativity and joy restored. I have often thought that the ideal would be to take one of these retreats each month and to spend thirty minutes to an hour a day in prayer.

- *Worship as you lead worship.*

This is one of the great struggles that most pastors face. It is very hard to actually worship while you are leading others in worship. I find myself thinking about the next act of worship, or my sermon, or the child that is crying, or a hundred other things related to the logistics of the worship service. Unfortunately that can mean that you as pastor never actually worship—you attend and lead, but you do not truly engage. And so, the very thing we tell our parishioners is essential for their faith, we do not pursue ourselves. Here's what I have to do. I choose the very last service of the day, and I make a covenant to actually be a worshiper at that service. I kneel in prayer before the service and ask God to help me to worship. I try to clear my mind of everything else and actually focus on the meaning of the songs we sing. I listen intently during the special music, closing my eyes to concentrate on the words and to listen for God to speak through it. It is amazing that, although I will have just completed six worship services, I feel so energized by this last worship experience.

- *Allow your sermon preparation time to be a spiritual discipline.*

On Mondays when I am doing my research for the weekend's sermon I try to approach this as an opportunity to grow in my own faith. I begin this time with prayer and invite God to teach me as I study. I look at this time of study as a wonderful blessing. How many people can spend five to seven hours in a week just reading and growing and seeking to know and understand God more clearly? When I approach my study from this perspective I find the experience most rewarding and enriching. This is something it took me ten years to discover, but it has transformed work into joy and spiritual renewal.

Let's switch gears for a moment and address the issue of moral failure. As a pastor you will encounter temptation. Your temptation may be toward hypocrisy—that is, telling others what to do without actually practicing it yourself. It may be sloth—an unwillingness to do the things you know God longs for you to do. It may be sexual in nature, or perhaps lying or stealing or practicing some form of addictive behavior. It would require an entire book to address all of these. You will be tempted. The question is How will you respond? Here are just a few basic principles I have tried to put in place to help me avoid succumbing to temptation.

- *Practice what you preach.*

It is so easy to challenge your people from the pulpit to do something that you know you yourself are not doing. You intend to do it. You believe in it. But you are not doing it yourself. Jesus had strong words for those who "command others to carry heavy burdens but do nothing to carry them themselves" (Matthew 23:4, my translation). I have, at times, preached what I did not practice. But I have made it a point to begin practicing whatever I have just preached. That is, I understand that sometimes my best sermons were the ones in which God was actually preaching the message to me. So I make it my aim to put into practice those things that I preach.

- *Be honest with yourself and, if possible, with your spouse or another confidant, regarding any inappropriate feelings you may have toward another person.*

You will have these feelings from time to time—it is normal. The question is, What will you do about them? Your calling as a minister and your ability to minister to others, including the one you feel attracted to, is jeopardized by such feelings. Whatever you do, do not tell the other person about your feelings; communicating your feelings to the individual is taking one step closer to acting upon them. You cannot act upon these things without doing serious harm to a whole group of people. A pastor or church leader must be honest enough to recognize these feelings. Talking about these feelings to one's spouse, if married (and if she or he is emotionally able to handle this) can have a tremendous and positive impact. In this you have enlisted the support of your spouse, and you have taken the secretive nature of the desire away, robbing it of its illicit power. If you cannot talk with your spouse about these things, or if you are not married, find another person who can hold you accountable—another pastor, a judicatory officer, or a close friend.

- *Do not put yourself in a compromising situation.*

Most people who fail morally put themselves in the situation in which they were likely to fail. I once knew a recovering alcoholic who would frequent a bar to order milk or iced tea. This is ridiculous. If you put yourself in a situation where you could compromise yourself, the likelihood is that one day you will. In the case of attractions toward another, do not spend time alone, or extended time even in a group, with the individual you are attracted to. Don't place yourself in a situation that could lead to a moral compromise.

- *Do not hire someone to whom you are attracted for a position with which you work closely.*

If you feel a strong attraction to someone who is applying to work with you, exercise extreme caution. This is simply good common sense.

- *Practice tithing.*

Our family has found that tithing helps keep our focus when it comes to material possessions. The higher our income the more our family is attracted to "stuff." I have to fight the materialistic tug that is such a part of our society. I find that the tithe is an important way to do this. As our income has grown with the size of our church, the percentage of our income that we are able to give away has increased beyond the tithe.

Life in the Pastor's House—Tips and Ground Rules

Some reading this are unmarried, but for those who are married, these are a few pointers I've learned along the way that have either helped me stay connected with my wife and children, or which have kept them from resenting the church and my ministry.

- *Take your day off—religiously.*

My day off is Friday. My aim is to do no church work on Friday. My wife and I often meet for lunch and a movie in the afternoons as a regular date, before the kids get home.

- *Take all of your vacation.*

In The United Methodist Church pastors are given four weeks of vacation each year (other denominations have similar requirements). This is an important benefit that compensates, in some way, for the extra hours, nights, and weekends that you spend in ministry. Use it! We take a two-week-long family vacation each summer and the rest is spent throughout the year. Nearly all of this is spent together as a family.

- *Take your spouse on continuing-education trips.*

When I am speaking at a conference across the country, or attending a continuing-education event, I will often take my wife, LaVon, with me so that we have a couple of days together. These have been some of the most wonderful times in our marriage. Since my airfare, hotel, and rental car are already paid for, the cost for her to join me is minimal.

- *Guard supper time.*

Most effective pastors will work three to four evenings a week, especially in their first twenty years of ministry. I have often worked this or more. But I do not schedule supper meetings (or do so very rarely). Instead, I aim to always be home for an hour or two each evening at supper time to connect with my children. If you have a meeting scheduled in the evening, consider coming home earlier than normal so you can spend time with your children.

- *Stay home with sick children.*

When our kids were small our church was smaller as well. I had fewer appointments and it was relatively easy for me to reschedule appointments when a child was sick, so I would stay home from work. I could read and study from home, as well as break away from this to care for the kids. This created wonderful bonding times and made up for some evenings away.

- *Be at your children's daytime activities at school.*

If I have enough advance notice I can usually plan my schedule around daytime events at the kids' school. This is one of the advantages to the pastorate—our schedule is more flexible than most. I am sometimes one of only a few dads who are present for daytime school events.

- *Talk with your children about your faith; solicit their ideas for ministries and sermons.*

My kids were my best resources for children's sermons when they were smaller. They had great ideas! I also try to find times each month to have an informal conversation with our children about their faith and mine. My hope is that even if they turn away from their faith as young adults (which I hope they will not do) they will never forget our witness and the joy and reality of our faith, and this will draw them back to Christ as they grow older.

- *Pray with and for your children every night.*

I am not always home at bedtime to pray with my kids, but every night, before I go to bed, I pray for them. Sometimes I kneel at the foot of their bed and pray for them. Sometimes I pray from my bed, but always I lift them up before God. I pray for my daughters and my wife several times throughout the day. This keeps them uppermost in my mind and actually deepens my love for them.

- *Take your children on church-related trips with you when possible.*

When I took a sabbatical leave in 1998 our family purchased a conversion van and a pop-up camper and the entire family was a part of my sabbatical study of America's large churches. When we would worship at various churches I paid my children

$1 each to write down comments from a "kid's perspective." I spent half of each day studying churches and the other half playing with my family. Late at night, after they had gone to bed, I would write up my reports.

- *Schedule time with your family just as you would for any other meeting.*

I have had times where my evening meeting schedule was completely full for weeks on end. When these times came I had to actually schedule time with my children in my planner, otherwise the church ate up all of my time.

- *Always ask permission to tell stories about your children, and never embarrass them from the pulpit.*

This is an important rule that they will appreciate.

- *Don't allow others' emergencies to control your life (see chapter 10 on pastoral care).*

Early in my ministry I missed too many events with my children while responding to "emergencies" that were not emergencies, and "crises" that could easily have waited until the next day to address.

- *Schedule premarital counseling sessions in the afternoons and wedding rehearsals in the early evenings.*

I already covered this in the section on weddings, but I will reiterate it here. Couples will come to appointments with the pastor at 4:00 P.M., thus freeing up your evening to spend with your family. And wedding rehearsals work nicely at 5:00 P.M. and if run well can be over by 5:45 P.M., giving you Friday evening with your family. You do not need to attend the rehearsal dinners and couples will understand if you will explain to them that you have a date with your children. If your children are grown or if you don't have children, attending a rehearsal dinner can be wonderful.

- *Spend time daily thanking God for your spouse.*

I find that the more I express appreciation to God for my spouse, by naming the qualities I love about her and thanking God for all that she is and does for me, the more in love I am with her. Try this, it works!

- *You do not need to attend all of the committee meetings.*

This comes as quite a shock to many pastors. If you have an excellent chairperson, and if you meet in advance, perhaps for lunch, to talk through the agenda, it is entirely possible to not attend some committee meetings at all, and to miss others occasionally when you have important events with your kids. We do have various staff people assigned to most of the critical committees in the church, but I only attend staff-parish relations committee meetings, and our church council meetings. (In addition I am involved in a number of ad hoc groups that come together around key events, and I will attend some of these meetings as well.) Beyond this I do not attend any of the other regular committee meetings. At the same time, there have been key issues that needed my personal attention and support at some meetings, and I am sure to be at these committee meetings when such an issue is coming up.

There is a careful balance that a pastor must strike between the church and the family. Churches don't experience rapid growth, or accomplish extraordinary things apart from a leader who, at some stage in the church's development, invests a significant amount of time and energy in the church's ministry. You cannot develop an extraordinary ministry in forty-five hours per week. But you can set up a plan to invest in your children's lives, spend quality time with your spouse, while leading your church, if you're willing to be creative.

EIGHTEEN

A Postscript and a Word of Encouragement

I have attempted, in this book, to communicate everything I have learned, both through my personal experience and through interviews and studies of many of America's most dynamic churches, about developing effective congregations. As I look back over the chapters I realize that there are so many topics that were never even mentioned. I suppose most of these will have to wait for another book. There are a few bits of wisdom that I cannot end this book without including, as well as a challenge to those of you reading this book who are my colleagues in mainline churches. So this chapter is a bit of a postscript.

Five Simple Truths

It is the pastors and church leaders who are willing to do what other pastors and church leaders are afraid or unwilling to do who will change the world.

Three words that should flow freely from your lips: "I am sorry."

Five words that successful pastors say a lot to their congregations: "I am proud of you!"

Never participate in conversations that tear down your colleagues or anyone else. It only reflects poorly on you.

Unfortunate but true: Most people do judge a book by its cover. Your appearance as a pastor or church leader can either enhance or detract from your ability to lead. Dress and carry yourself like a high-quality leader, whatever that looks like for your particular community. In addition, demonstrate confidence in order to inspire confidence in your leadership.

Two Questions I am Frequently Asked

How Much Land Does a Church Need in the Twenty-first Century?

Considerably more than at any time in the past. Cars are a fact of life, and often a family will bring two to worship. You can fit, at best, one hundred parking spaces into an acre. Ideally you are striving to have no more than eighty cars per acre to allow for adequate green space. If a church has thirty minutes or more between worship services, one parking space for **There is no turning back from the trend toward larger churches.** every two seats in the sanctuary should suffice (this takes into account simultaneous Sunday school and worship). If the church has a very large adult Sunday school attendance and Sunday school is simultaneous with worship, more parking may be needed.

In addition, churches in the twenty-first century will be offering ball fields, recreation and wellness centers, and outdoor gathering places. There will also be a move back to having cemeteries located on church property. All of these take space.

It is inadvisable for any new congregation to begin with fewer than twenty acres. If the church is in a location where worship attendance could grow beyond fifteen hundred per weekend, a site of forty acres or more should be considered.

One additional factor to consider in looking at a potential church location is the access and egress—the roadways into and out of the site. Many churches have overlooked this, with disastrous consequences. A traffic consultant should be employed to help the church analyze any potential church locations to see what kind of traffic load the surrounding roads and entrances and exits to the church can handle.

One church I know owns fifty-five acres of land, but there is only one road into and out of its property. The traffic load for this road will likely handle two hundred cars per half hour exiting and entering, yet the church plans to have several thousand per weekend in worship attendance. Though the church owns enough land to support the parking requirements for the projected worship attendance, the exit could not support these numbers. In addition the one exit is near a hill, which creates a dangerous problem as traffic is leaving the church.

Is the Trend Toward "Megachurches" Going to Pass?

There is no turning back from the trend toward larger churches. The largest churches in the United States today are bumping up to the twenty thousand in worship per weekend mark, and show no sign of slowing down. Each year another church grows beyond ten thousand in worship attendance per weekend. The megachurch is here to stay, and there will be far more in the future than there are today. Here's why:

1. Megachurches are able to offer a large array of choices that no other church can offer.
2. Megachurches are able to offer a quality of services and staff that is difficult for smaller churches to match.
3. Megachurches are able to offer facilities that make possible ministries that would be impossible in any other setting. These include athletic, educational, youth, singles, and young adult ministries meeting in spaces designed to meet these needs.
4. Megachurches have the opportunity to have a tremendous missional impact on the community and the world. This continues to fuel the growth of megachurches.
5. Megachurches exist primarily in larger cities that are able to support their size and growth. What is true of megachurches is true, relatively speaking, in the larger churches in your community. The trend in most places will be toward larger congregations with more choices, offering high-quality ministry and multiple options for small groups and outreach.

6. Further strengthening the position of large churches in our society is the fact that large churches are able to attract and keep high-quality pastors and staff members. Long tenures among pastors and staff strengthen churches. Large churches often keep their pastors for decades, and staff tenure is among the highest in the church world.

Just as Wal-Mart, Target, and other large retailers are here to stay, so are America's larger churches.

What does this mean for your church? I am not certain. Small churches will need to pursue excellence in ministry and focus on, and highlight, their strengths when threatened by larger churches starting or moving into their communities, just as small businesses have had to adapt and specialize in light of Wal-Mart's move into county-seat towns.

Small churches have much to offer that large churches cannot. Small churches offer a personal relationship with a pastor, an opportunity to know everyone in the church, a tremendous support community, and the chance to be involved to a very high level in the church.

Many healthy small churches can and should embrace the vision of becoming innovative, regional churches in their own areas, and begin making plans to become the church that reaches its community and the surrounding countryside. The information in this book was aimed, in part, at helping small and medium-sized churches to reach their full potential in service to Christ and in reaching nonreligious and nominally religious people.

Your church has incredible potential, whether you are a small rural church or a large downtown church. You are the body of Christ! You have the power of the Holy Spirit at work in you! You have the greatest mission of any organization in the world! And at least half of the population in most parts of our country is nonreligious or nominally religious. Not all of the ideas you've read in this book will work in your church, but many will. Not all of the principles you've learned in this book will apply to your church, but many will. As a leader, and as a church, commit yourself wholly to Christ. Invite the Holy Spirit to empower and guide you. Love and lead your people. And dream bold, God-sized dreams!

A Special Word to Mainline Church Leaders

This book was written for pastors and church leaders of any denomination, in the hope of providing helpful principles and concrete ideas to allow your church to become all that God intends for it to be. But I have a special interest in and passion for mainline churches. Over the last thirty-five years, mainline churches have seen a tremendous diminution of the vitality of their denominations and their role in society. These historic leaders of American Christianity have faced year after year of losses in membership and worship attendance. Most of these denominations are 20 to 50 percent smaller than they were in 1965, a decrease that came while the population in America increased by 69 percent.

> **This book was written to say that it is possible for mainline churches not only to survive, but to thrive.**

A multitude of books have been written on the reasons for this precipitous decline, and the critical changes that must be made in our denominations in order to see a turnaround. This book was written to say that it is possible for mainline churches not only to survive, but to thrive. It was written not from the perspective of a sociologist, a seminary professor, a denominational official, or a church growth consultant, but from the perspective of a pastor who has seen the power of the mainline approach to the gospel, and how hungry twenty-first-century people are for this perspective.

This book is not filled with theories and untested ideas, but instead is a record of what has actually worked in one local church, with the key concepts and practices that led to unprecedented growth within a mainline church in the last thirty-five years, a growth that outpaced most of the nondenominational and conservative megachurches in their first ten years of existence.

We experienced this growth not by ignoring our historic mainline roots and theology, but by embracing them, and translating them for a new generation. When asked by my fellow United Methodists to enumerate our "secret" I can honestly say that much of our approach at Church of the Resurrection is simply an adaptation of what John Wesley did 250 years ago.

All of this is to say that the death knell that was sounded for mainline Christianity may have been sounded a bit prematurely! In fact, *I am persuaded that the next great awakening in American Christianity will happen among the historic mainline denominations*, and, though I am of course a bit biased, I believe that United Methodists stand a chance of leading the way!

Mainline Christianity has been likened to the "sleeping giant" of American Christianity. It has often forgotten its historic faith, its passion for the gospel, and the power of its traditions. But if it can remember who it is, and the gospel it has been entrusted with, amazing things are in store.

There are at least five reasons why I am persuaded that mainline Christianity can once again be a tremendous force for the kingdom of God, and in fact is *perfectly poised* to "serve the present age." These five reasons certainly apply to The United Methodist Church of which I am a part, and I believe they relate to most other mainline churches as well.

1. The Union of the Evangelical and Social Gospel

Mainline churches have a historic commitment to *both* the evangelical gospel and the social gospel. We have sometimes forgotten one or the other of these perspectives, to our detriment. But at our best we hold dear both the personal, life-transforming salvation that comes through a relationship with Jesus Christ *and* the challenge of the social gospel, inviting persons to apply their faith and love of neighbor to the real world, and to issues of profound importance in society. We offer opportunities for people to meet Jesus Christ in prayer, worship, and discipleship, and to live the love of Christ in mission and ministry to a broken world, while offering care and help for people in need. Mainline Christians, at their best, might be described as "evangelical liberals" or "liberal evangelicals" in the most positive sense of both of these words. And this approach is a gospel that will reach and preach to twenty-first-century people!

2. The Union of the Heart and the Intellect

John Wesley was described by some as a "reasonable enthusiast." That term describes the very combination that so many people are looking for when it comes to faith. Mainline churches, at their best, bring both a rigorous and serious intellectual approach to the gospel, coupled with a passionate, heartfelt and experiential faith. We have the most educated clergy in Christendom. And those clergy should have had their "hearts strangely warmed" by the power and touch of the Holy Spirit. It is when we ignore either the intellect or the heart, or both, that our churches, and our proclamation, become cold.

3. The Union of Tradition with an Emphasis on Cultural Relevance

In many nondenominational churches it would seem that Christian worship did not exist before 1985. The great hymns of the faith have been lost to so many. The power of symbol and liturgy has never been experienced by millions of Christians. The Protestant mainline, along with our Roman Catholic and Orthodox brothers and sisters, is the great keeper of these traditions. They are part of our treasure—the church year, the holy days, the symbols of the faith, the profound significance of the sacraments. All are elements of our heritage and worship life that we offer the world. At the same time our churches were birthed out of a deep desire to make Christianity both apostolic and culturally relevant. This, too, is part of our heritage. Our hymns were written to speak to the people of the day. Our forms of worship were indigenous and opened the door to the sacred for common folk. We have historically sought to bring the gospel to the people in a way they could understand it, and then apply it to their daily lives. We are a church that embraces and brings together both traditional and contemporary expressions of faith and worship. We are this kind of church, at our best. Unfortunately, too often we have

> We have offered grace so freely that we have lost a sense of personal accountability and sometimes the challenge of Christ, after he offered grace, to "go and sin no more."

forgotten the meaning of our symbols and traditions, and simply continued to practice them as though by rote, until our traditions have become dead "traditionalism." We have forgotten our founders' cries for relevance and indigenous worship and surrendered this ground to others. But when we remember our heritage, and hold both tradition and cultural relevance together, and when we help others understand the power of our traditions, we have an approach to the faith that is compelling and that has a depth that speaks to twenty-first-century people.

4. A Compassionate and Grace-filled Gospel

Among the greatest and most appreciated attributes of mainline Christianity is its emphasis on grace and compassion. Our churches seldom preach condemnation and guilt, but instead a faith built around grace, and God's mercy, and a compassion and love for all people. We welcome all persons into our flocks. We are sensitive to the feelings and the pain of others. (Some critically call this "political correctness," but if being politically correct means being thoughtful and compassionate toward others, and expressing profound truths in ways that do not build walls and unnecessarily hurt people, then we are guilty as charged.) When I ask unchurched people to tell me what they don't like about church and organized religion I typically hear that churches are judgmental, hypocritical, and that they excel at making people feel guilty. Some churches may, in fact, be like this, but not typically the mainline churches. Unfortunately, in our zest for offering grace, we have too often forgotten Dietrich Bonhoeffer's profound first chapter of *The Cost of Discipleship* and his lessons on the costliness of grace. We have offered grace so freely that we have lost a sense of personal accountability and sometimes the challenge of Christ, after he offered grace, to "go and sin no more." If we can offer grace and demonstrate compassion, while lifting up high standards and an invitation for people to repent and experience the life Christ intends for them to know, we will have a gospel that today's nonreligious people have a deep longing to hear.

5. An Elevation of the Role of Women in the Church

Mainline Christian churches have often led the way, particularly in the last half of the twentieth century, in embracing and elevating the role of women in the church. While we were criticized for our use of inclusive language with regard to human beings in our hymnals, liturgies, and Bibles at the time they were introduced, today nearly all of society uses inclusive language in the newspapers, television, and in education, when referring to people. Today women may serve in nearly any role anywhere in society, except in a large number of conservative churches where women still cannot teach Sunday school (except to children), serve on staff (except in women's ministries or sometimes children's ministries), or serve in any key leadership positions in the church. This approach to the role of women in the church will become increasingly out of step with society in the next twenty-five years. At the same time mainline churches have, with varying degrees of success, fully empowered women to serve in the church in any capacity, including the role of pastor. This has strengthened our churches as women bring a wonderful balance and perspective to leadership in the church that is missing when they are excluded. Our senior leadership team at Church of the Resurrection is made up of three women and three men, and this is a blessing to our church. Two of our five ordained pastors are women and they are exceptional. And many of our top leadership positions in the church are filled by women.

As with each of the other four characteristics of mainline churches, there are dangers with this strength too, which can actually cause it to be a hindrance rather than a help in reaching our society. Allow me to explain.

When I was a youth director years ago I found that I could not reach the young men if the only leaders they found when they came to youth group were girls and women. I had a large number of girls who would volunteer for leadership positions in the youth group, but only a few guys. As long as there were not many boys serving in leadership, it was difficult to attract other guys to youth group. Once I began personally recruiting guys, and developing them as leaders alongside the girls, we began to reach young men.

In many of our mainline churches, the last twenty-five years saw the advent of women in leadership. This was a blessing. But in the process, many men abdicated. In many of our mainline churches church became something for women. Mothers came to church; fathers stayed at home. Women sang in the choir; men sat in the congregation. Our women's groups were very strong and wielded great influence in the church; our men's groups lagged far behind. Women taught our children in Sunday school; men were absent from education. The only remaining bastions of male leadership were the finance committees and the boards of trustees and sometimes our staff-parish relations committees. Even these began to change in the last ten years.

I mention this to say that unless we develop both female *and* male leaders in our churches, we will find it difficult to reach the twenty-first-century male. Once more we have capitulated in this area to others who have filled the vacuum we left with movements like "Promise Keepers" and whose churches take a very opposite view of men by placing them solely in leadership. We must find a way to reach and attract males into leadership, alongside women, if we will reach our full potential as mainline churches.

If we can find ways to appreciate, encourage, and reach men, while continuing to embrace and lift up the role of women in leadership, we will have a wholeness and balance in our churches that twenty-first-century men and women will demand of their faith communities, a wholeness many other churches simply will not be prepared to offer.

There are currently at least seventy-five thousand congregations that make up what have been traditionally called mainline churches. Many of them will close in the coming decade. Many others will continue their slow descent toward oblivion. But something very exciting is on the horizon for many of our churches. Church of the Resurrection is but one of hundreds, if not thousands, of mainline churches that are beginning to see nothing short of a modernday revival, reaching a new generation of people who had been lost to our churches in the past, and developing ministries that are changing the world. *This book was written with the hope that your church might be added to their number.*